Deidre Lingenfelter

KRISTINE CARLSON is an international bestselling author and a leading expert on love, success, grief, happiness, and parenting. Along with her late husband, Dr. Richard Carlson, Kristine has experienced phenomenal success with the Don't Sweat the Small Stuff series. She has been featured on national radio and television broadcasts, including *Today*, *Empowered Living Radio*, *The View*, and *The Oprah Winfrey Show*.

"A heartwarming, important, and powerful book for all moms (and even some of us dads). Thank you, Kris, for continuing the beautiful legacy and philosophy that have made the Don't Sweat books accessible and life-changing for millions of people around the world, including me. This wonderful new addition to the series is an empowering gift for moms, dads, and families everywhere!"

—Mike Robbins, author of *Focus on the Good Stuff*

"Kristine Carlson aims the time-tested and highly effective Don't Sweat philosophy toward motherhood in this insightful, entertaining, and empowering book. A must-have for all moms!"

—Steve Maraboli, author of *Life, the Truth, and Being Free*

"*Don't Sweat the Small Stuff for Mums* is a godsend for moms of all ages. If you have ever felt alone, isolated, crazy, or lost as a mom, you owe it to yourself to get this book. As a mom myself, I felt delighted to read a book filled with such honesty, advice, warmth, and love. Kris is a compassionate, inspiring guide to help us navigate the wild waters of motherhood. She has taken the Don't Sweat the Small Stuff series to the next generation of greatness with this book. Wow!"

—Amy Ahlers, author of *Big Fat Lies Women Tell Themselves*

"As a mother and cofounder of a nonprofit that works with parents and youth around the world, I know this book is timely and will truly bless the world."

—Yvonne St. John-Dutra, cofounder of Challenge Day
and author of *Be the Hero You've Been Waiting For*

"*Don't Sweat . . . for Mums* offers page after page of sage and gentle advice, the kind we all crave braving the enormity of being a mother. You will have at your fingertips a guide that will remind you, night or day, that motherhood was never intended to be mastered and you are not alone on this journey."

—Maryanne Comaroto, author of *Great Relationships Begin Within*
and CEO and founder of SHOMI, LLC

"Kristine Carlson has done it again and I thank her for her words of wisdom and practical advice. We women need as much support as we can get as we juggle our careers, families, home lives—and yes, taking care of ourselves. For all of us who are just too busy trying to do it all, this book belongs by our bedsides for comfort reading and sage advice. Thank you, Kristine!"

—Jennifer Seibel Newsom, CEO and founder of MissRepresentation.org

"Kristine Carlson has given readers a collection of powerful essays that invites moms to enjoy their family time more and to create happy homes where children can thrive and grow into successful and happy adults."

—Marci Shimoff, author of *Happy for No Reason*

Don't Sweat
the Small Stuff
for Mums

—••—

Kristine Carlson

BANTAM
SYDNEY AUCKLAND TORONTO NEW YORK LONDON

A Bantam book
Published by Random House Australia Pty Ltd
Level 3, 100 Pacific Highway, North Sydney NSW 2060
www.randomhouse.com.au

Published by arrangement with Hyperion, 114 Fifth Avenue, New York, NY 10011

First published by Bantam in 2012

Addresses for companies within the Random House Group can be found
at www.randomhouse.com.au/offices

National Library of Australia
Cataloguing-in-Publication Entry

Carlson, Kristine, 1963–
Don't sweat the small stuff for mums / Kristine Carlson

ISBN 978 1 74275 552 6 (pbk.)

Parenting.
Mothers – Attitudes.
Women – Psychology.

649.1

Cover design by Chica Design
Internal design by Jennifer Daddio/Bookmark Design & Media Inc.
Printed and bound by Griffin Press, South Australia, an accredited ISO AS/NZS 14001:2004 Environmental Management System printer

The paper this book is printed on is certified against the Forest Stewardship Council® Standards. Griffin Press holds FSC chain of custody certification SGS-COC-005088. FSC promotes environmentally responsible, socially beneficial and economically viable management of the world's forests.

FSC
www.fsc.org
MIX
Paper from
responsible sources
FSC® C009448

I dedicate this book to my devoted and loving mother,

PATRICIA ANDERSON

Thanks, Mom, for giving me
a wonderful example to follow.
I love you!

CONTENTS

INTRODUCTION

✿ When I was asked to continue the popular Don't Sweat series with a book for moms, I felt honored and unsure at the same time. It would be the first book to be added to the series, and Richard Carlson, my beloved late husband, the author of the *Don't Sweat the Small Stuff and It's all Small Stuff* book series, would not be here to celebrate this addition. I was also questioning how could I write a book summarizing what it has taken me a lifetime to learn. In fact, *Don't Sweat the Small Stuff for Mums* is truly a paradox because we moms seem to naturally sweat every detail every day for our families. We are logistics managers, the chief executive decision-makers of our homes; nurses; chefs; coaches; and guidance counselors, and many of us do all of this alongside a full- or part-time career, while being married or single—each of those statuses bringing with it its own challenges. It's no small task being a mom today.

The more I thought about it and the more I spoke to other moms, I realized that a Don't Sweat book for mothers was exactly what I would have wanted when I became a mom more than twenty-two years ago. As I began scratching out a list of ideas for this book, I was surprised by the many feelings about motherhood and my own experiences that came to me. I am now on the other side of raising a family. My nest is empty and my children are grown. Both of my girls are in college now; my youngest daughter, Kenna, graduated from high school last year and my oldest daughter, Jasmine, will give birth to her second son in a few months. So that makes me a grandmother, too. I have been just about every kind of "mom" now. I was happily married to Richard Carlson, my soul mate and life partner, for twenty-two years, and am now a widow (five years already), which makes me a single "Nana." My children were fourteen and seventeen when he passed away suddenly. Going through that was in itself quite a journey—but that's a different book.

As I worked through this writing endeavor, I realized that there wasn't much of anything new I could share, but instead I found that the time-tested and proven methods of getting through life as a mom with grace, confidence, and an empowered attitude still work. As with my other books, this process was both introspective and therapeutic, as it brought back to me emotions and feelings that had gotten lost in the untidiness and activity of raising children. Feelings of fear and even regret arose as I thought—often—how I wish I had baked more cookies and cooked more family dinners; that I'd had more patience and been a better listener. I wished that I'd always been wise and responsive and found just the right words when I needed them.

And that maybe I was not a good enough mom to write this book after all.

My whole identity as a mother was in my face, and as I reflected back, I had to acknowledge that I am not, even now, the quintessential mother who has done a "perfect" job. I am, however, a woman who has evaluated many of the things that I have done right, and those that I could have done differently. I look at my girls today—caring, loving, strong women—and realize that I got most of it—the small stuff and the big stuff—mostly right.

Each chapter treats an issue that I was concerned with at one time or another. (I would have loved to have had a book like this as a young mother and would have appreciated the hard-won wisdom that comes through trial and error.) In other words, everything in this book is tried-and-true and built on the Don't Sweat philosophy that is all about taking personal responsibility for your own happiness, keeping life in perspective, and being gentler with yourself and others while accessing your inner peace and wisdom. I am grateful to have relived my journey as a mom by writing this book for you—although I have to admit that writing about motherhood is about as much fun as motherhood itself (sometimes). Being a mom is a big job, with small and memorable moments calling on our patience and building our character every day. Every day brings a new set of lessons and tests laced with small joys and a large purpose. Truth is, it's all pretty overwhelming and daunting, when we are just starting out. We know that raising small children will exhaust us (we don't know just what that means, however, until we're there) and that teens will test us. But it's like any journey you take—it happens in small steps one right after the other.

This book is broken down into one hundred short, bite-sized chapters to read and think about at your leisure (did I say "leisure"?). It's meant to give you a few new perspectives, ideas, and reminders of things you may already know, and perhaps even encourage you to make some small changes. When I started out my mom career, I wasn't sure about a lot of things that I know to be true now. If you are reading this book, chances are you're already doing a great job as a mom.

I share this book, my memories, and my experiences with the hope you will find inspiration for your heart. And even though I know you take care of the small stuff, I hope this helps you remember not to sweat what you don't have to. Make the changes you need to in order to live the most conscientious, peaceful, and loving life you can. As the mothers of this world become more joy-filled, the heart of each home will be full of love and kindness, and the ripple effect of that will be simply astounding.

Treasure the gifts of life and love,
Kris

THERE'S NO SUCH THING
AS A "PERFECT" MOM

✺ Just for a moment, take this in fully, and say it to yourself: "I don't have to be the perfect mother." How many times have you carried the burden of thinking you have to live up to some ideal "fairy-tale" image of a good mother? One who is relentlessly kind, patient, wise, nurturing, good-tempered, inexhaustibly energetic, a fine cook and home-maker, a multitasker—that person few of us have ever actually met who "can do it all"? That's not to say that, as mothers, we shouldn't strive to be the best examples for our children that we can be, but we do them a disservice when we hide our mistakes, don't allow them to see our flaws, or don't apologize when we've been wrong. We need them to see the world as multi-dimensional, and that means the people in it, as well. Give yourself permission to be authentic and to express yourself completely as a mom. When we do so, we relieve not only our own stress to live up to impossible standards, but we help our kids to see that they don't have to be perfect, either. When we make space for imperfection and mistakes, we give our kids a chance to deepen themselves and to become more true to themselves and real as they grow up. Abandoning perfectionism is such a relief for us, and them.

One of the ways in which we can show our humanness is to own our mistakes and bear witness to humility. If you hold yourself too high on the proverbial pedestal, not only do you alienate your kids, but also it can be a long way down when you fall. If, on the other hand, you admit to your errors or become more transparently yourself, you not only avoid a fall but also teach your kids important lessons. Many times, we make excuses or blame others when things go wrong instead of accepting responsibility for our shortcomings (and I emphasize "short"-comings). Transparency allows your children to see you exactly as you are, and promotes the deepest kind of connection. It is also a show of true self-confidence and self-love that you accept yourself as you are, in all of your humanness.

Oftentimes, when our kids push the limits of our patience, we blow. Whether we are dealing with a toddler or a teen, as parents we set boundaries for our kids, and when they cross those boundaries we issue consequences. But sometimes we get so caught up in the moment that our anger or frustration overwhelms our sense of perspective, and we go too far. We say things like "You are grounded for the rest of the school year." When dealing with children, especially teens, it's very easy to overreact (although I had a few quarrels with my little ones, too). Once we've cooled down, we see it, but we're usually too embarrassed to make amends, to say that we spoke thoughtlessly or even cruelly or to roll back a consequence that really didn't fit the crime. We fear that we'll look silly; that we'll lose our authority and that our children won't respect us again. But there is a better way. You can admit to your kids that you lost it, and say: "I'm not apologizing for giving you a consequence but I am sorry for how I lost my patience and for what I said (or the severity of the consequence)." You are showing your child that life is filled with mistakes and imperfection, and that we don't always learn from the things we do right. Oftentimes, we learn from the things we do wrong. Maturity is about taking responsibility, and knowing that no one is perfect all the time, and that we can always come back from a mistake. Teach them that all perfection really means is that you've recognized an opportunity to take steps to do or be better. In the real world, that's truly all we can do.

Richard and I use to joke together: "I'm not okay. You're not okay. But, it's okay." As we show our kids that we are infallible and willing to make amends for our mistakes, we show them a vulnerability that aligns us with the rest of humanity. What a relief! Shed your cloak of invulnerability today. Doing so will let your uniqueness as a parent shine, while giving your kids permission to be human, too. It's a great feeling to know that we are all perfectly imperfect, just as we are.

2

NOURISHING YOUR SPIRIT FIRST

❀ "Take time for yourself" may seem like an old adage, but it's never been more necessary than for today's woman, as we often juggle a busy schedule that includes a full-time career and an intensely structured family life. If you're anything like me, you've asked the question, "Where do I fit into this picture?" more than once since embarking on this family journey. You are where all things start in your family. While it may take some ingenuity to create the space in your day, taking time to nourish your spirit is the single most important thing you can do for the well-being of all.

There is no job that fits the term "overworked and underpaid" more than that of being a parent. Our commitment is boundless, and we carry our responsibility 24/7. Then, too, we are trying to be loving partners and competent employees. We're firing on all cylinders, and it's a marathon. Raising children will occupy a full quarter of our life expectancy. These are also our best years—when we have the most energy and our capacities are at their peak. You want to do it all, and to do it right—to be the best you can be in every role you have. To do this, you need to create the space to nourish and take care of *you*, and to make sure that becomes a valued part of your day.

I've always believed that the very early morning hours are a woman's best time. That time of day before the house starts moving, when the light is pink with the sunrise and the air fresh with dew, belongs to you. There is nothing better than to get your day off to a peaceful start. No matter what ages your kids are, you can create a few minutes of time and space for yourself for meditation, walking, reading the newspaper over a cup of freshly brewed coffee, or just watching the morning sun burst into day. It will carry you through the hours ahead and nourish your spirit. A practice that works well for me includes waking up at least one hour prior to my family. I sit quietly while sipping fresh coffee or tea, and take in the stillness. Then I always do ten minutes of stretching and inspirational reading. Sometimes, I turn on soft music as part of my meditation. I also spend some time thinking about the things I am grateful for. Then, I pull out a notepad or my laptop and make notes for the day; this clears my head and helps me to feel calm before I begin it. What lies ahead is on paper; my mind is uncluttered. Sometimes I will journal at this time, too. Mostly, I spend some time noticing the peaceful place that exists within me, a place that sustains me all day long. I breathe in sunlight and breathe out tension. Breathe again; sunlight in, tension out. Nourish, nourish, nourish.

An early morning ritual reminds you that the day is buoyant and full of possibility. Anything wonderful can happen as light chases away the dark night sky. It is a reflective and contemplative time when you can do your best thinking and feel the peace that can ground you while you move through your day. Then, when your family rises, you can be present with a positive good feeling and an attitude of gratitude. Remember that loving yourself and nourishing your spirit is loving the family you care for, and there is no better way to start your day than connecting with the beauty inside you.

3

GROWING YOUR GARDEN

On a recent trip to Peru, I was struck by how happiness seemed to be a way of life for the indigenous people. In these beautiful village communities, simplicity seems to be the order. These families live on their farms, close to their land, trading their art and growing their own fruits, vegetables, and grains.

Back home in America, as I reflect back on the many things we did as a family, I think about the wonderful times we spent together tending to our family garden. I still smile as I remember my little daughters playing on the railroad ties that framed the garden as if they were balance beams, while we planted rows of squash, lettuces, carrots, and tomatoes. Together, we tended and harvested the results, and the joy of sending the girls outside to pick tomatoes for our dinner salad or gathering fruit from our fruit trees (apple, apricot, and kumquat) is among my fondest memories.

I believe in growing a garden as something you and your children can nourish together. There are fewer more gratifying family activities than tending and harvesting nature's bounty. As the plants develop from seedlings into mature produce, every day in your garden is a chance for the kids to bear witness to the cycle of life and to our ecosystem at work. And bringing freshly pulled lettuces and vegetables from the garden to your table is just a wonderful way to enjoy meal preparation for many months. You don't need a backyard or acres of land to grow something edible. Using a window ledge, you can plant a sample of herbs, a single tomato plant, or a pot of strawberries. It doesn't have to be sophisticated. All you need is water and sunshine. Looking at the big picture of life from a spiritual perspective, I like to think in terms of nature's metaphors to gain a clearer perspective on my vision of family. As life unfolds, most of us will agree that we couldn't have anticipated the realities and many challenges we face day in and day out while caring for a family. I have often thought of my own family as a grove of trees that all share the same land but are uniquely different—all bearing our own fruit while growing together side by side. In the same turn, I have thought of conscious parenting much like tending to an organic farm, where every plant and flower is a different shape, size, and color, just like the members of your family— all needing to be cared for individually and collectively.

How we care for our garden determines how it will grow. Our garden, like our family, will do well if we give it the right conditions from the start. Just like a garden, you tend to the needs of your family as they arise each day. We can make it our intention to do our best as parents and provide a loving environment in our home that is clean, well rooted, nutrient rich, and safe. The plants may need gentle pruning like our children do now and then as we remind them with discipline that there is acceptable and unacceptable behavior. We provide structure and boundaries so that our kids can reach a safe maturity. We lovingly care for them emotionally and physically, often picking them up when they fall down and offering our guidance as they learn to solve their own problems, much as we stake tomatoes to give the stalks support. We send them out into the sunshine and nourish their health by encouraging activity and play. We protect them from harmful influences and predators. We celebrate their individual accomplishments, allowing them to shine brightly and bear the fruits of our labor and love.

As you make it a family project to grow your garden, you can also use this metaphor to gain a larger perspective. Remember that the basic needs of a family, like a garden, are simple. No matter what state yours is in, all it really requires to sustain itself and thrive is consistent attention and loving care.

4

EMPOWERED "MOM"

It's true that knowledge is power, but being an empowered "Mom" is all about what you do with the knowledge you have. You may gather perspectives from many different sources, but at the end of the day, you must be the expert who chooses the direction of your family.

The experts in our children's lives—their doctors, teachers, and coaches—not to mention the wisdom of family members, friends, and clergy who have "been there"—are essential resources to us as we raise our families. Gathering information and educating yourself is critical to good decision-making. But no professional degree or years of personal experience is ultimately more important than your own intuition. As you navigate through the sea of opinions and ideas, you will also notice that the "experts" sometimes conflict with each other, and sometimes with your goals and values. So you will need to use your critical thinking and problem-solving skills to analyze the advice and information you've gathered. Then remember that you are the "Decider." That is because no one is a better expert in the matters of your family than you.

I always took the issues that would arise with our girls seriously, whether they included health, school, friendship, or emotional well-being. They were important to my girls and therefore they were important to me. I would read about an issue and solicit ideas and opinions from people I respected. Then, I would do exactly what I taught my kids to do. On paper, I would list the pros and the cons of each of the available options. I would evaluate each, either alone or in combination, choose one, and then create a step-by-step action plan in the form of a flowchart. I also maintained a separate spiral notebook or computer file that included all the resources for that one project, so I could locate references easily.

I've seen a number of excellent examples of what it means to be an empowered "Mom." I've particularly observed how parents of children facing special challenges have become strong advocates for them. If you have a child with a learning, emotional, or developmental disability, you are the ship that cannot sink, because your child is the passenger. If you cannot rally to the job, there isn't anyone else who will.

I was in the classroom the day our children's preschool teacher pulled my friend Jeanine aside for a word. When she returned, Jeanine, who is normally so composed and unflappable, appeared shell-shocked. She trembled as she told me: "The teacher thinks Ben has autism." That day, Jeanine began a journey of a thousand steps. There would be triumph and sorrow from battles won and lost as she sought information about autism and services for Ben. At that time, fifteen years ago, there was very little published about autism. Jeanine was a fighter, however, when it came to her son. She spoke to doctors, educators, therapists, and lawyers, and even battled the public school district to get Ben into a special school program that could meet his needs. She delved into everything from nutrition to special neuron-feedback therapies. She became familiar with the Americans with Disabilities Act, empowering not only herself but also her son. All these years later, it is clear that the early intervention propelled by Jeanine's devotion has led to a far better result for Ben than what would have been the case had she passively followed the literary advice of the "experts" and that of the school district's recommendations for the education of her child.

Parenting requires us to be leaders. An empowered mom must have the courage of a warrior and the persistence of a bull. When she seeks solutions that work within the framework of her family, she exercises her right to choose best, and she knows without a doubt that she is the one to make these decisions.

5

MAKE SPECIAL MOMMY
AND ME TIME

When we brought Kenna home from the hospital, it didn't take Jasmine long to discover that there was a huge disconnect between her imaginings of Big Sisterhood and the messy reality of the actual experience.

Richard and I talked about how important it was to continue to give Jazzy special time with each of us and especially, because I was nursing Kenna, to make "Mommy and me" special times a priority with Jazzy, to help her transition from being the only child to being a sibling.

When you use this helpful transition tool, be sure to emphasize the specialness of your time spent away from everyone else in the family—especially the new sibling. Try to make at least ten minutes every day to be alone together; you will be surprised how much of a difference even a little time can make. Tell your older child how much you love spending special time together. It reinforces your bond, helping the child to feel secure, special, and loved. Remind your child there will be many times when you will share these special moments, and that that will never change.

For your part, having your special mommy time gets you out of the whole family scene (let's face it, some of it isn't all that much fun) long enough to see how nice it is to be with just one child at a time, adding more joy to your parenting.

Sometimes our kids don't know how to verbalize that all they really want is some of our attention. A girlfriend, Kay, was sharing her frustrations that her nine-year-old son, Sam, doesn't like to do his homework alone and wants to sit next to her while he does it. She was busy in the kitchen, and he kept engaging her with questions that she knew he could answer for himself. She became frustrated and resented this habit he had fallen into. He finally blurted out "You're so busy all the time. I never get to see you. All I want is to spend some time with you." She stopped and realized that he just wanted her attention. She responded by saying: "How about I answer your questions, you get your homework done, and then we play a game, or make lunches together?"

As your kids get older and you spend less time together, taking them on a special outing or a special weekend or vacation really helps you hone in on raising your child's self-esteem while it enhances the unique relationship you have with them. When you are alone together, you can focus on those things that are of interest to this particular child, and you can also enjoy the common interests that you both share. One friend has older parents who live in another state. She visits them regularly and when she does, she makes a point of taking just one of her children with her at a time. The long drives are great opportunities to engage in uninterrupted conversation, and the alone time one sibling spends with the grandparents also deepens that relationship.

While we spent a lot of time together as a family, I came to cherish those occasions every week when I would whisk one girl out the door for an ice cream date or a special shopping trip to pick out new shoes for a school dance, or for a day at the park. Family love is built on individual love. A celebration of each relationship in your family helps to boost and strengthen the whole, while providing great memories for all.

6

BUILDING YOUR FAMILY TEAM

❀ Sometimes it can be overwhelming when you feel 100 percent responsible for everything happening in your home. Practicing the art of delegation and team-building can make all the difference. There is no reason for you to do everything. Start thinking of yourself more like a captain of your ship who needs a crew to set sail, and your family team will be the wind beneath your sails.

A friend of mine is a lawyer with a busy practice and three very active boys. While her husband is a hands-on dad and a great support, there is simply no replacement for Mom. Studies show that women think more long-range and are better planners than men; they keep the calendars and make sure that there is toilet tissue paper in supply. They are somehow the ones who know where to find last season's mittens when the first snow falls; they are also better at striking items off of "to do" lists. And, as any mom will tell you, they are the lighter sleepers; you know, the ones who somehow always hear when a child is calling out in the middle of the night. So when I asked my friend how she managed to create balance in her life, she explained to me that when her boys were younger and she was overwhelmed, she added more help to her family team.

Now, we all have different resources and budgets, and life is certainly easier when one can hire a nanny or a housekeeper. But there are other possibilities of finding help when you are creative in your team-building. Even your family dog can be considered part of your team. When Jazzy was little, I would put her in an area where I could keep an eye on her with our golden retriever and a ball while I folded laundry or prepared dinner. You can imagine what a perfect pair they were, both loving the same game and irrepressibly passing the time in entertainment and exercise together. Looking at our dog as a part of the family team and as a playmate for Jazz gave me just the break I needed to do my chores.

Your team may consist of you and your co-parent, but it also includes people like your pediatrician and your child's teachers and coaches. If you are feeling overwhelmed and unsupported, try to build a community of people, including friends, family, neighbors, and hired help, to assist you.

If you are a working mom, think in terms of what you need from a family helper. You may need support with after-school driving, or to have someone help organize your kids' homework when they get home. You may want someone to stock your groceries, or you can take turns with a friend doing a warehouse club store run for each of you. There are few ways for ten-year-olds to make money, as they aren't quite age-ready for babysitting, but you may know a young person who would love to be a mother's helper and play with your toddler while you are in the house, or give you a hand with household chores. Neighborhood children can make great household helpers, and for your children it can feel like having an older sibling, without the rivalry.

It may be worthwhile to employ a responsible adult to help you out, understanding that your time is valuable, too. If paying or bartering with someone frees you to do other necessary things—or even to rest, which is necessary to your own physical and mental well-being, and thus to your family's—then you ought to consider it. Think of the extra assistance as an investment that will be temporary. For most of us, these years of raising small children truly fly by. And eventually, your older children will become part of the team, too.

As you look at the team you have, perhaps there is a way you can ask for more specific help from the people who are already in place in your life. My daughter babysits on occasion for a family. When Kenna started college, she began to help the high school–age children in this family with their papers and homework, via e-mail and Skype. Their arrangement is a great example of taking a closer look at the skills of your team members, and seeing how, with some management and delegation, you can take something off of your plate.

You may be the crystal in your family clock, but give yourself permission to ask for help. Take a closer look at the people in your life and the possibilities for how you can create more harmony in your life by delegating. As captain of the ship, set your course so that it can be smooth sailing for you and your family.

7

MOVING THROUGH PMS
AND LOW MOODS

Most days begin like any other, but once in a while we have our "off" days—we are, after all, just human. There are times our immune system is low and we may be coming down with a cold, or we're just overstressed with too much to do. Some days, we're just "hormonal" or low—we wake up with raging PMS. It doesn't make you a terrible person or a bad mom to have those emotional ups and downs, but it takes some awareness and self-compassion to get through them as gracefully as possible.

Navigating our individual well-being while raising a family can be challenging. The nature of motherhood seems to dictate that we take care of everyone else before we take care of ourselves. How many times have we made lunch for the kids while forgetting to make ourselves a sandwich, too? (I can't count the number of times I ended up eating the toast crusts off my girls' plates after they'd left for school and calling that my breakfast.) We give our kids a time-out when they need it, but somehow we forget ourselves, and that we might need a break, too.

A wise mom knows she needs to take care of herself. It's a little like those announcements we hear every time we get on a plane. In the event those oxygen masks drop down, we're told, always put on yours first before assisting your children with theirs. I always thought that was counterintuitive. Wouldn't a mother's first instinct be to take care of her child? Then I realized that no, we are of no help to those we love when we are also ailing. In other words, we need to breathe, too. In terms of family time, this means we need those small respite breaks that allow breathing time for us.

Sometimes, Richard would leave us for a business trip, or on an isolated writing retreat, or a much deserved few days away to have a mini-vacation and two or three days' time to spend with his best friend, Ben. It would always amaze me to discover that these days fell on the week before my period. I often laughed as I gently accused him of sheepishly planning to be away during that time in my cycle. I would say to him jokingly, "Are you kidding me? You are going to go on vacation and leave me with the kids and my PMS? I make no guarantees what you may find when you get home." I was kidding, of course, but I have to admit that these times when he was gone and I was suffering from symptoms of PMS were highly stressful. My mental and physical balance shifted during this time, and I wasn't as emotionally grounded, empathic, or as capable of dealing with stress as calmly as I otherwise was. I had a short fuse.

So I learned to warn my daughters ahead of time by saying it straight: "Girls, I could very well turn into a monster mommy today, and I'm sorry that I am extra tired and sensitive; my temper is short because I am about to get my period. Please don't take my mood personally." When Richard was home, I would warn him, too. We both knew that I was more sensitive around my period. Everyone got the point: They knew not to be hurt when I snapped at them for the small stuff, and that most of the things that annoyed me during my PMS week were not considerations any other time.

It's okay to cut yourself some slack during these low-mood times. In fact, I learned to anticipate them. I would do everything possible to stack the cards in my favor by creating extra space in our family routine that week, which would help me to feel more grounded and help me return to a peaceful center. I would often schedule a babysitter, trade time with a friend with children my girls' ages, or prepare meals in advance—strategies that would give me some extra quiet time to nourish my extinguished spirit. I would go for a hike, run, meditate early in the morning, or take an evening bath. I would pay closer attention to doing the practical things within my control, such as eating well, getting more rest, drinking plenty of water, and exercising—even if I felt as if I was dragging. It also really helps to remind yourself that this is not the "real you." The "you" under the thrall of PMS is forgivable—and yes, even lovable.

Being aware of your natural mood cycle will give you the opportunity to smooth over the roughest edges. Making some minor adjustments ahead of time that stack the cards in favor of your own well-being will help you and your family through these more turbulent days.

Remember that even the best mothers are going to lose it now and then. We're not always going to be on an even keel, but a sound sign of mental health and positive self-care is how quickly and gracefully we move through those low points to return to our inner peace and nurturing wisdom.

8

SURROUND YOURSELF
WITH GREAT MOTHERS

If you surround yourself with other moms whom you respect and can share ideas with, it makes it so much easier to be that great mom yourself. As mothers, we are inspired by each other, just as artists receive inspiration from other sources—after all, we are engaged in the "art" of living and happy parenting. Making the effort to get together on a regular basis will create a supportive and trusting network with which you share notes and vent frustration at the many challenges that arise. Moreover, these informal "Mommy and me" groups will free you from the feelings of isolation and loneliness that can so easily happen in our widespread communities.

I just visited a mommies' group the other day, and I noticed how community support and camaraderie enhance the joy these women experience as they laugh together about the things that come up with their kids—things that might otherwise leave a mom feeling very lonely and low. I listened as they discussed everything from teething and night terrors to cracked nipples to diaper rash, and they shared the invaluable wisdom of having so many resources. Each of them had read different books and shared ideas that had worked for them in specific situations.

New mothers do seek community and find each other by striking up casual conversations in the park or at the pediatrician's office. They can find each other through friends of friends, on church or library bulletin boards, and through community centers that have outreach programs. While I think it is important to be around moms who have children about the same age as yours, it's also nice to have friends with older children "who have been there, and done that." It's also important that you surround yourself with others with whom you share similar values and a similar lifestyle, too.

Moms who are working out of the home may want to participate in a group with other working mothers, so that you can discuss day-care possibilities, mutual child-care support, and time management for routines that help you get that extra chance to enjoy your kids or to make time for yourself. At the group I attended, Caren told me that she is inspired to keep Emily on a schedule that came from another working mom who also works from home. When their daughters were ready to give up their naps, it threw a wrench into the day, as the mothers lost those extra two hours they were accustomed to having. They both introduced "quiet play hour" instead. As part of their routine, the little ones come home from morning day care, have a nice lunch with Mommy, and then go to their rooms and have imaginary time with their dolls, or dress-up. All of the women I spoke to agreed that having the support of other moms who were dealing with the same stresses helped them to stay inspired and upbeat in their approaches.

Often we don't have extended family living close to us, and in many cases, our friends become our chosen support. No matter what your situation as a parent, I encourage you to surround yourself with other like-minded moms. Having a support network is truly important; it really does take a village to raise a child, and I encourage you to find your tribe.

9

CUTTING OUT THE FAT:
NEED VS. WANT

As Baby Boomers, we were raised under the illusion that living a good life meant living well. We felt the drive to monetize our achievements so that we could acquire a bigger house, a faster car, take nice vacations, and dine out. The bigger the better—or so the emphasis went. Earn it and spend it. A high standard of living was an entitlement, and so spend we did.

It wasn't difficult to be caught up by a cultural ideal that urged us to acquire more instead of being satisfied with what we had, but truthfully, it didn't make many of us feel very good. The pressure of acquiring that big house and lifestyle turned out to be terribly stress-inducing, because no matter how much you had, someone else had more. Abundance, we discovered, was a poor substitute for contentment, particularly if it was built upon debt; and satisfaction turned out to be elusive.

And then the freight train that was our economy jumped the track. Living as we do today, each of us making all sorts of economic adjustments in the way we save and spend, has given us an opportunity to create a new model for family life that may just make our children's lives richer—in a more lasting sense—than growing up during an economic boom could ever do.

I think it's important to look at your household's economic arrangements with your children as soon as you feel it is age-appropriate. Help them to understand the difference between needs versus wants—those things that are absolutely essential to living (food, clothing, shelter, electricity, heat) and those things that we may like very much, but don't require (ice cream, candy, iTunes, trips to the mall). Prioritizing needs vs. wants, and talking about your dreams as a family, can help make the necessary adjustment to your budget while still maintaining your family vision. Stephen Covey recommends in *The 7 Habits of Highly Successful Families* that you write a family mission statement. This is a great idea because it enrolls your family in the intention of creating life as you would like it to be, showing kids that it is altogether possible to work together to achieve your dreams (a college education, for instance).

An important part of this process is the opportunity to include your kids, so that they may feel personally invested while also learning the basics of budgeting and planning, or what is known as financial literacy. Your family mission statement may include taking a hard look at just the things you really need, and the economies you will all have to make to afford them. Sit down together as a family and reveal what resources are available and decide what your priorities are going to be as a unit, and also as individuals. For example, consider proposing that each family member for the next year empty his or her change at the end of the day into a central kitty. That money, you will see, accumulates quickly. You might decide to jointly save toward a family vacation, or with the idea of making a contribution to a charity related to children or to a cause of special significance to your family. Children may also be asked to make their own lists of needs and wants: Each child may consider wearing their shoes until they no longer fit or are worn out rather than purchasing yet another pair of shoes they don't really need but merely happen to fancy. Or, each child may be able to choose just one extracurricular sport or activity per season instead of packing their schedule with so many commitments that they become meaningless as well as unnecessarily expensive. Perhaps stops at the local pizza parlor can be cut back, or skinny lattes can be made at home. Turning lights out, turning the heat down, and limiting cable television channels also help children to have a better understanding of need vs. want.

There is really no better way for kids to learn about money matters than by giving them their own to manage—i.e., an allowance. When you give your child a certain amount of money, whether it is for the week or the month, and clearly explain what costs you will continue to cover (food, gas, school-related expenses, pharmaceuticals, personal grooming), and what costs must now be assumed by the child (lunch, snacks, movies, music) you are helping your child to understand that money doesn't grow on trees and that life is about making choices. They will learn to plan for essentials, and to do without those things they can't afford. An allowance not only will spare you from dealing with a child's most annoying requests ("Pleeeaasse???"), but will also give them practice in making good decisions. However you decide to initiate your children into the world of money matters, make it a family affair, and do it together.

10

THE WRITING MUST BE
CLEAR ON THE WALL

When Jazz was nine months old, being new to all this parenting stuff, I called my parents one day in frustration and said, "I feel like she is running the show here. We are jumping through hoops for her and she's not even walking or talking yet! Something is wrong with this picture; I don't know how this happened."

My mom and dad laughed, as all grandparents do, at our inexperience as new parents, and then stated the obvious: "That's because sweet little Jasmine *is* running your house. You need to let her know by your actions what the boundaries are. You must be in charge of your house. The writing must be clear on the wall."

I listened carefully and knew they were right. We began to regain some measure of control by learning to set clear boundaries, gently but firmly. It took about three months to undo the habits we had formed. At first she cried, but she soon settled into our way of doing things—most of the time.

Whether you are dealing with a two-year-old or a teenager, this strategy is perhaps the most important thread to carry through in effective parenting. And, having lived through both the terrible twos and the testing teens, the only thing different about them is the level of sophistication in how your child tests the limits and boundaries you set. Whether you establish the rule that your toddler needs to eat his meals in his high chair, or must eat dinner before dessert, or that bedtime is at 8 p.m., or that your tween must do chores before she heads out to meet her friends to go to the mall on the weekend, or that teens must complete homework before having phone and social media time, the boundaries must be clear.

Jazz became a high school cheerleader as a sophomore, and some of her friends on the squad were upperclassmen who were already driving. The first summer we had to deal with her being in a car with young drivers really worried us. I had read about the distractibility of young drivers; I had heard about the terrible accidents they had while texting or having too many passengers in the car. I couldn't sleep until she got in at night. She had a strict curfew, as well, which we considered to be the very liberal hour of midnight. About three weeks into summer, she was fifteen minutes late coming home, even though I had warned her of the consequences if she didn't arrive on time.

As Jazz walked in the door, I was seated at the dining room table waiting for her. She saw me and asked, "Mom, why are you up?" She could see that I was mad. I said, "What time is it right now?" She looked at the clock: "It's a little after midnight." I asked, "What time are you supposed to be home?" She responded with that impatient and somewhat defensive pout parents of teens know so well, "C'mon, Mom, I'm just a few minutes late." Without raising my voice, I answered: "For every fifteen minutes you are late, your curfew will be shortened by half an hour. Your new curfew this summer is eleven thirty p.m." I stood up and walked out of the room and went to bed. And she wasn't ever late again.

When the writing is clear, so are your boundaries. If your limits are reasonable and applied with consistency, the world becomes a safer and more secure place for your child. Whether it's little ones or older children, your "no" must mean "no," and your "yes" mean "yes." When you teach them that you say what you mean, and you mean what you say, you are also modeling integrity and reliability—and therefore helping them to become the adults you hope they will be.

Despite their protests ("Everyone else does it! You are the meanest mom on the planet!") kids know intuitively that they aren't ready emotionally, spiritually, or developmentally to set their own boundaries. As you lay down the groundwork for healthy discipline, stay a bit ahead of the game. That is, it's easier to set up structure ahead of time than to backtrack later, and it's fairer for your kids to know what to expect. I learned to really spell out the boundaries, dotting the I's and crossing all the T's. That's where the wall comes in: If you leave a hole in your boundary, it's easy for them to find an opening to jump the fence. Ambiguity makes it more difficult for you to respond without being defensive. When your rules and expectations are clearly stated, they know that when they blow you off, they blow their freedom.

When it comes to raising kids, consistency and love is everything.

Your words must be backed up by swift and clearly defined consequences. While I don't believe in do-overs, I do believe in redemption and second chances. I always have wanted my kids to know there will be a next time and that I believe in them. Nonetheless, when you are tested—and you will be—remember that your words are important as a warning, but actions always speak louder to kids.

11

PRACTICE BREATHING
BEFORE YOU SPEAK

You'll notice that the importance of breath has been highlighted in several chapters. This is a reflection of its significance in bringing ourselves to a peaceful place inside, and I've found that this is especially so before we speak. Breathing deep from the belly is a great way to access your inner wisdom and bring yourself into a calm resolve that is conducive to healthy responses. In my life, I have found this particularly important to do when I have been agitated by my kids. Don't they always know how to push our buttons?

Think about it: How many times have you wished that you had thought before you spoke? Well, thinking isn't always the whole story or what you need to do first. Sometimes, in fact, our thoughts become triggers that contribute to our agitation and then we react rather than respond. That's because your internal barometers and weather vanes are found in your feelings. These gauges will show you where you are in the moment. In order to access these feelings, you need to breathe and check in with yourself. The process of conscious breathing allows your parasympathetic nervous system to calm down your thinking brain—the part of your brain that processes feelings and brings you to a place of reason—to kick in. Conscious breathing can help you to rein in what might otherwise be an explosive reaction when a calm and centered response to a situation from your inner source of common sense is desired.

Even now, when my girls come to me with their problems, complaints, or concerns, if I don't remember to pause and breathe, I almost always say the wrong thing, and the conversation ends badly. Nothing invites drama and hurt feelings like a reactive response. To avoid this, I start to take deep belly breaths in and out while I'm listening. Sometimes, I don't even say much, because I realize that all my daughters really want in this moment is to be heard. Conscious breathing helps me access presence, so that I can listen from a place of love and compassion.

During those times when they ask for advice, I try not to speak until I am sure that I've accessed that place of wisdom and quiet confidence, and am not speaking from fear or anger. When we speak from fear, we are being reactive; when we speak from a place of love, we are being responsive. Many times, if you are fearful and you react to your children without breathing first, breathing will calm you and bring you into the moment. We can see in nature how animals often startle before they react in fight or flight. You will see them stop suddenly and stand erect and aware, sensing the energy around them, before they react and respond. Conscious breathing works very similarly.

Most people are unaware of their breathing patterns. Try to be mindful about yours. Focus your attention on your belly, and breathe in through your nose. As you take in your breath, first your belly expands and then as you inhale more deeply, your chest expands. Then, exhale all the air out through your mouth as your belly goes back in, returning to normal, and letting go of any tension you are feeling. Taking several breaths like this will help center your brain so that your thoughts are clear, and then you will be more likely to adjust the tone of your conversation accordingly. The practice of deep belly breathing can also be useful throughout your day, whenever you feel overwhelmed or stressed. It will really help you to access more peace inside, and connect you with the inner wisdom that reconnects you to your compassion and love.

12

CHOOSE HAPPINESS AND PEACE
OVER STRESS

As a mom, you cannot wait for the day to happen when all of your "lists" are complete with tidy check marks. Whether it is our "wish" list or our "to do" list, we know that our plates will never be completely clean and our in-baskets will not be empty. Having a perspective on happiness begins with having an attitude that says, "I am going to do what I can today, and let go of what I don't get done, because it will still be there tomorrow." Unless you have the house-cleaning fairy show up in the middle of the night to keep order in your home, there's always going to be something to do. Phyllis Diller said, "Cleaning the house while children are growing is like shoveling the snow while it's still snowing." It's endless and ongoing. So you have to just put those household chores on hold and don't miss an opportunity to have an experience with your kids because you are neurotic about being organized, tidy, and clean.

"I choose happiness and peace over stress" is an affirmation to live by. We all know there is plenty of stress attached to your life as a mom, and if there was a video camera in every home, many times it looks like Mom is putting out fires. In order to keep stress to a minimum and to maximize our moments of joy, it really helps to keep it all in perspective.

When my friend Rebecca's children were three and five, she received a life-threatening diagnosis. Life changed very suddenly as she embraced her treatment. Thankfully, she survived. Rebecca shares her experience of how getting this news and overcoming her illness gave her greater perspective on what she valued most, which was time with her kids. She said: "The small things that used to seem so important, like running my household well, small stuff like folding and putting away and straightening up after the children, no longer mattered. What mattered most was grabbing an umbrella and walking in the rain and allowing my kids to jump in the puddles and play in the mud. My experience of life has been enhanced by knowing—*really* knowing—that every day and every moment matters."

Another way in which you can choose happiness over stress is to identify your small stuff with your kids so that when it comes up, you can let it go. Not everything has to be a battle. Children often have different ideas about how they want to spend their time or how they want to express themselves in the world. Your daughter may want to wear purple rain boots with her ballerina tutu to the grocery store, or your nineteen-year-old son may tell you he's thinking of getting a tattoo. A wise mother once said to me, and it stuck: "Choose your battles. If my kid wants to spray-paint his hair purple one day, well, that's just fine. I have plenty of battles to fight with him, and his hair is not permanent, but gives him the power of choice he's looking for right now. If I can see this as a small way to give him power, then I can be free of the need for control. It's also easier for him to hear me when I try to talk him out of something I think is truly wrong for him."

Our kids give us many opportunities to see what matters. What matters isn't necessarily the thing that looks best; sometimes what makes us happy doesn't always make us admired. Which way would you rather have it? And, what is it you want to remember when you look back: the spontaneous and unstructured moments when your child climbed into your arms to cuddle, or the couch pillows that didn't get fluffed or the floor that didn't get vacuumed that day? When we choose happiness first, we preserve our energy and enjoy our life with family more. We don't have to receive life-changing news to gain perspective. We can wake up to each moment and remind ourselves there's no contest when it comes to letting the small stuff matter more than the big moments we are blessed to experience with our kids.

13

TALKING TO TODDLERS
ABOUT SAFETY

✿ I'm not sure if the world isn't as safe as it used to be, or we are just more aware of the things that can happen, but every mom wants to make sure her child is protected from harm. The challenge lies in teaching our kids about safety in a way that makes them alert without making them afraid. This type of teaching can help children understand the boundaries of appropriate social and sexual behavior, and their right to protect their own bodies.

One of the things that will help you accomplish this is to talk to your child about appropriate behavior from other people, sometimes known as "good touch/bad touch." This type of conversation considers those persons, including older children as well as adults, who are larger and more sophisticated than they are. We teach our kids not to talk to strangers, but we also know that sometimes it's the people we trust who turn out to be the most dangerous predators. That is why we need to have thoughtful and caring conversations when our children are small, and to carefully explain to them that no one—not their day-care provider, babysitter, teacher, or athletic coach; not other children; not even clergy or extended family members—may touch them inappropriately. These gentle conversations need to take place early.

When one of our daughters was three, we took her for a routine doctor's visit. As the pediatrician was moving through his checklist, he reached down to lower her panties. Before he could get them to her knees she grabbed his hands, pushed them off, and pulled her pants back up, firmly saying: "No! Don't do that!" The doctor startled and looked at me in dismay, not understanding why she would do that. I explained that Mommy and Daddy had instructed her that private parts were only for her to look at and touch. Even after I explained the difference that in this instance, with Mommy present and that the doctor was just going to make sure that she was growing as she should, she continued to refuse the exam, clearly embracing the teaching that her body belonged to her and demonstrating a clear understanding that her private parts were private. Knowing that she was healthy, I decided to honor her boundary and enforce her personal right to choose what felt appropriate to her in the moment. I was, in fact, proud of her that at even her very young age, she could stand firm to effectively communicate her personal boundaries.

We live in a world where our children's innocence is sometimes stolen from them. It hurts us—bewilders us—to think that we need to teach them to protect themselves, but we do. One important way we can help to keep our children safe is by teaching them to tell the truth no matter what. In many abuse cases, a perpetrator will use fear to intimidate a child into secrecy because children don't know that it is safe to tell the truth about what happened to them. It is vital they know that if any person ever violates their private boundaries or makes them feel "icky" and not right, they can come to you. It must be clear that nothing bad will happen to you if they tell, and certainly nothing bad will happen to them. It must be clear that they are safe coming to you, no matter what. Be sure your child has a plan to come to you, and knows that they can feel safe telling you about *anything* that may make them feel unsafe.

14

YOUR HOME IS YOUR HAVEN

There's no place quite like home. I remember that feeling as I walked in the door after being away at college and coming home for the first time. It seemed as though I was walking right into my mama's arms and loving embrace. Home to me was a place I always wanted to return to, and it has been such a joy to pass on the same good feeling of a safe and nurturing haven to my children. As a woman, you are the heart of your home and all things extend from your gathering. My own mother did such a lovely job at providing warm comfort with her distinctive taste, which was traditional and refined but extremely comfortable. Home carries so many personal meanings and layers. Practically speaking, it is your family retreat, the place where your meals are eaten and your head lands safely in bed at night. On a deeper level, it is where the tree of your family finds its nourishment and its roots. Home, with its aesthetically pleasing spaces and adornments—the artwork, weavings, mementos from family travels, and special heirlooms passed down through the generations—is the physical representation of the beautiful life you've created. It represents your aspirations and your truth.

The many spaces of home reflect your family as a group, but also as individuals. Just as you set aside play space for your children or adorn the refrigerator with their efforts at self-expression, and as your spouse or partner may have made a "cave" to retreat into (a shop, a wine cellar, a studio to play music in, or a garage in which to tinker with a car), I encourage you to create a space that is sacred to your own personal inspiration. You may have to be creative and open a small alcove or a closet for a desk or an altar. Your space could be defined with a table and meditation pillows stacked on the floor. Perhaps there's a spot for a writer's desk in your bedroom. Your space could be in your bathroom. Wherever you choose, make it personal and yours, a place to own where you can feed your soul.

A girlfriend of mine started a business but also loves to work out and paint. She converted her garage into a work and "be" space where she also placed her treadmill and a small TV. Her space is shared on one side with children's toys that are stored for the season or clothes being stored while the next child ages into what the other has outgrown. She defined her space with a large rug over which she placed her desk and inventory of products in neatly organized crates. Her easel stands on its own with her paint caddy beside it. And she took an old yard sale sofa and threw a sheet over it, and tucked in the corners to give it a shabby chic look.

We are not all inclined to be so ambitious, and some of us have no extra space anywhere. When the four walls are truly all you have, think about creating virtual space for yourself. A laptop or a desktop can transport you anywhere, including into a sacred place or domain that can give expression to your personal interests just as surely as any physical reality can. However you are able, make a "home" within your home for yourself, and make it your haven, however you choose. It's pleasing to create a nest and an inspirational place for you and your kids to return to again and again.

15

MOM TAKES A TIME-OUT!

✿ There is plenty of advice in this book about raising tweens and teens, but getting through the toddler and elementary years with your small ones really tests your emotional and physical reserves.

I was recently talking with a mom I met at the playground when I was with my grandson. She had three children with her, ages eighteen months to six years. She was telling me that she didn't know how to get a break in the day for herself because neither one of her older kids took naps any longer. I nodded, as I remembered how sad I was when my girls no longer napped. But I had put a strategy in place for myself because I knew that as the day rolled toward that five o'clock hour, if I didn't rest and regroup, I would be as cranky and useless as a tired toddler myself. If Richard was traveling, which was often the case, it would have been very difficult to maintain my patience through the evening routine because I would have been simply exhausted. Giving myself a "time-out"—a short break that allowed me to catch a power nap, meditate, listen to music, read a magazine, or otherwise "zone out"—restored me and frankly, allowed me to keep my sanity.

I made every afternoon around two o'clock my time for rest or meditation. My kids, then four and six, were still young and needed me nearby, but did not need my full eyes-on-them-all-the-time supervision. I also devised various little games for them, brought out picture books from the local library, or simple projects or puzzles and video programs they could watch to occupy themselves and safely pass the time. Some days, they played together quietly. (Note: When young children are old enough to give up their naps, they are old enough to take simple instruction, thankfully! Older children can watch younger children and call for you if needed. Of course, very young children cannot be left alone! Sorry, Mom's Time-Out may have to wait a little longer.)

I had a nice large open area near my bedroom where I spread out a colorful blanket for them, with soft throw pillows. They knew that when the blanket came out, this signaled it was Mommy's Time, and that they needed to stay on the blanket for a short while. I would close my bedroom door and take my twenty-minute respite. When I emerged, the girls were happy to see me, and I—rejuvenated now—was happy to see them. They always knew that when I emerged from behind the door, there would be a treat; we'd sing a song together; we'd put on music and dance; we'd go to the park. The day that stretched ahead of us was new again.

I have a friend with three active boys ages seven through fourteen, and believe me, she needs her time out. She has a sign she places on her door that reads: "Not now, I'm meditating." She puts her iPod earpiece on late in the day every afternoon before she begins to prepare dinner, and her boys know that if she's interrupted—or if they begin to fight with each other—there will be consequences. This is an idea that works very well with older children. It's good to lead by example and show that self-love is allowing yourself some time for being still, to rest and re-group.

Mommy's time-out was an opportunity for me to hit my shut-off button to refuel so that I could operate for the rest of the day full steam ahead.

Balance and harmony can be restored with small increments and practices that nourish your inner peace and your ability to stay present and patient. If you are overworked every day and frustrated at the lack of time you have for yourself, taking a time-out is imperative toward maintaining your well-being and vitality.

16

BUILDING RAPPORT
WITH YOUR CHILD

✾ From the moment you bring your baby home, you begin to build a rapport with your child that grows like a snowball over a lifetime. It's easy to fall in love with an infant, but building rapport with a teenager is quite different. Strengthening your relationship with your maturing son or daughter requires you to focus your intention.

Having rapport means that there is openness and trust in your relationship that are built with consistency in your interactions. There are times where you may feel in synch with your child, where communication is easy and you are mutually responsive to one another, with good rapport. Other times, you may feel defensive with one another and your positive good feelings may weaken. While your role is to be the teacher and guide, you must know when to back off and just listen without judgment—especially if you want your kids to feel comfortable sharing their thoughts and feelings with you. Building rapport with your child starts at birth, but is like a wheel that is constantly turning, where each interaction builds on another, creating and forming deeper trust.

I watched my friend in the kitchen with her nine-year-old. When Olivia haphazardly threw something in the wrong recycling bin, Lisa gently corrected her. When she did so, she used humor and a kind tone. But then she continued, "Olivia! Honey, you know you are the one who taught me about recycling, and I have been noticing that our recycling has not been going so well. Now the compost is . . ." Frankly, it really did sound as if she was about to launch into a lecture. While Lisa was still speaking, Olivia placed her hand on her mother's, with a firm grip to get her attention, and in a soft but surprisingly authoritative tone, pulling her closer so she could look into her eyes, she said, "Mom, Mom, Mom! I hear you. Just show me next time." Lisa abruptly stopped, both of us laughing at Olivia's precociousness. Their good rapport carried Lisa and Olivia through the moment. I said to them, "That was really great, Olivia. And, Lisa, you will be so fortunate if she says, 'Mom, I hear you,' years from now!"

It's not always easy to have good feelings flow with our kids, and all relationships go through their bumps and bruises. Rapport shifts and changes as your kids do, and you can find new ways to strengthen the common ground you stand on by attempting to see the world through their eyes and finding new ways to engage in their worldview. Whether it be through having a sense of humor, a project you work on together for school, a meal you cook, or a sport you practice, spending quality time talking together and listening to one another while doing something you both enjoy is what builds a solid foundation. As you bond with your child, it's easier to navigate the strains that follow when you must set a boundary and discipline a child. It is far more likely to have the desired outcome when the understanding between you is based on affection and compassion, as well as respect. Remember, your goal as a parent is to have your kids listen to you with as little conflict and hurt feelings as possible. When we build good rapport, we can have some of our best interactions while showing up truly joyful in our parenting.

17

YOUR FAMILY'S HEALTH BEGINS
AT THE GROCERY STORE

We've talked about how important good health is to our family. I've interviewed many moms and asked them what their deepest desire is for their sons and daughters. Among the many qualities they wish for, strong healthy lives is always at the top of their list. Most children are born with robust natural health and vitality that gives them a good start in life. But we also need to acknowledge that the environment impacts what happens to them afterward, and so do we. While as individuals we can't control the air they breathe and the chemicals that pollute the soil where vegetables and fruit are grown and cows are fed, there are choices we can make as parents to create a healthful environment at home. We can buy organic products, and we can be careful about how we stock our food pantry. Every time you visit the supermarket to buy your groceries, keep in mind that your family's health begins at the store, and you have the power to choose well.

We know that childhood obesity rates in our country have steadily risen. When children vastly exceed the normal weight for their age and height, their chances for leading those good long lives are shortened as surely as by environmental chemicals. That is because childhood obesity often starts children down the path to serious health problems that were once confined to adults, such as diabetes, high blood pressure, and high cholesterol. Children who are obese also suffer from low self-esteem and depression.

We also know that it's natural for children to store some fat while they are growing, but by feeding your family a balanced diet of lean protein, dairy products, vegetables, whole grains, and nuts, your children will naturally balance out when they undergo their growth spurts. It's also critical that you stock your cupboards with healthy, low-sugar snacks. Sure, processed or junk foods are convenient for you, and kids like them, but they are loaded with empty calories that deplete energy and pack on the pounds. As an empowered parent, it's up to you to lead, and to lay down the law for what comes into the house and goes into your children's bodies.

One thing to remember is that preparing a healthy meal is a form of love, but that food itself is not love. Here are some healthy suggestions to follow as you shop:

- Stay out of the middle aisles and cruise the perimeter for all the good stuff. Your basic food groups are all there—fruits, veggies, eggs, dairy, and meat. You may have to meander into the middle for legumes and grains.
- When buying snack foods, choose baked chips, nuts, raisins, and things like apples, peanut butter, hummus, carrots, cottage cheese,

string cheese, and yogurt. Keep assorted nuts and trail mix around the house. Make your own granola bars and healthy cookies with raisins and nuts.

- Don't skimp on dessert. You never want your family to feel deprived. Serve dark chocolate and berries. Buy sorbet or frozen yogurt instead of ice cream. And when you bake, use less sugar and butter than the recipe calls for. You can probably cut these by one-third, and the baked goods will likely turn out fine.

- Start the day with a healthy breakfast. Breakfast not only jump-starts the metabolism, but also prevents you from feeling famished later, which leads to overeating at lunch or dinner.

- Read labels and look at cholesterol, sodium, and sugar content. (Be wary of breakfast cereals that are loaded with sugar.) Avoid saturated and trans fats. Make it a practice to keep up with nutrition guidelines, as standards are always changing.

- Practice portion control! Your kids don't need to eat as much as you think. Encourage them to slow down when they are eating and they will feel satisfied with smaller portions.

- Since refined white sugar turns to fat, we don't need much of that, either. There are many healthy sugar substitutes.

- The American Heart Association says that our kids aren't eating enough fruits and veggies. Pump up the meal plan with plenty of fresh produce. Introduce new vegetables to your picky young eaters, and reward them when they try something new.

- Think: Fresh is good, and organic is even better.

- Don't assume that because a package says "low-fat" that it means "without fat." Low-fat foods are often overprocessed, too, so limit those and stick with all natural ingredients as much as possible.
- Stay away from polyunsaturated fats. Use light cooking oils such as canola, safflower, and olive oil. Choose real butter over margarine, but use it sparingly.

Make healthy eating a family project. Kids learn their habits for life when they are young, and carry them into adulthood. Model good eating habits and they will follow your lead. Love your children by being conscious about what you buy at the store, put on the table, and put into their lunch boxes. If your kids are struggling with obesity, see your pediatrician and a nutritionist, and learn how to make better food choices. The eating habits you establish now with your kids are likely to be the ones they teach their own children. That makes family health a wonderful generational gift!

18

UNDER-PROMISE AND OVER-DELIVER

As I began writing this chapter, my original intent was for this to address working moms, but then I realized that this is an idea that all moms ought to consider. The strategy of under-promising and over-delivering sets things up so that your children have lower expectations and are always pleasantly surprised when the unexpected happens. Actually, this is a great strategy for all of life, isn't it? Makes us look pretty good when we show up bigger than expected, and we can really feel good about that.

We have a personal "trust fund" that is built from the power of our word. To build trust, we have to stick by our words. If you aren't going to deliver the goods, don't make the promise. Although our children are very unconditionally forgiving, if they are continually disappointed by the excuses you make for not being present in their lives when you say you will be there, they will eventually grow to not trust what you say. It doesn't work well to break your commitments by explaining yourself: "I know I told you I would be there, but I just don't have time today to be at your game or tennis match or dance recital because I have a meeting or have to take your sister to the doctor or something important has come up. But I promise you next time . . ." After a few times, your kids will get the message; their take-away will be: "You can't trust me, and you don't matter enough to me, to prioritize my time to show an interest and be committed to what you are doing."

Working mothers must deal with the fact that for more than forty hours a week, they just simply can't necessarily command their own schedules. All of us, regardless of how and where we spend our day, can't be in more than one place at a time, and if you have multiple children, well, everything multiplies with them. This scheduling dilemma may be frustrating at times; at times it may even bring you to tears because you know where you would want to be, if only you could. But this problem bears with it opportunities for ingenuity and creativity. You may not be able to be "Room Mom" for your daughter's third-grade class, for instance, but you can bake cupcakes and contribute to the holiday parties. As you lay out the calendar, look at it with your kids and emphasize the times you will be present. "I won't be able to attend the science field trip, but I will be at your baseball game or dance recital." If you have a partner, spouse, or car pool driver to pick up your kids after school on a regular basis, surprise your children whenever you can and pick them up yourself. And don't forget, you don't have to be guided only by the days the calendar says are important, you can make any day special. Slip an affectionate note into your child's bag or homework folder. If they have a cell phone, send them a loving video or voice message. Remember, you can choose to make any day special, just by showing up and being present, in person or by way of a small gesture.

The same is true with raising multiple children with multiple activities. You can't be at everyone's match, but you can divide your time equally. You may be at the beginning of one child's game and then scoot off to attend the end of the other child's. If there is more than one parent in your family portrait, set it up so that at least one of you goes to most games. Then, when both of you show up and it's not expected, your child's excitement will be palpable. Be sure to stress the things you are able to attend, and then make your rate of attendance 100 percent perfect. Show up unannounced when you can. As you under-promise and over-deliver, everyone wins and, most important, you build trust. Your actions will speak the unspoken message to your kids: "I love you, and I will be present whenever I say I can."

19

FIRST, NOT LAST, ON MY LIST

Of all the challenges you face in parenting, balancing being a parent with the needs of your romantic relationship with your partner can often be the most difficult. Once the excitement and adrenaline rush of bringing a "new" baby home wears off and you get into the trenches of infant care, with nighttime feedings and diaper changes, it's easy to let the romance in your marriage or partnership slide into sleep-deprived oblivion. Making your partner first on your "to do" list, and not last, will help you keep your priorities in line and will also be the salvation of your loving connection. As our dedication to our children in *Don't Sweat the Small Stuff in Love* reads: "To our children, Jasmine and Kenna: the greatest gift we have to give you is the love we have for each other."

As I was leaving my gym, I was speaking with another mom, and she mentioned that she barely had any libido anymore. She laughed when she said: "You know, with everything on my 'to do' list, my husband falls at the very bottom. I just don't have the energy for sex at the end of the day. He's the one thing on my list that is manageable and negotiable." (I was wondering how he felt about that.)

In your family unit, your kids are the product of the two of you; as a couple, you were first. In our household, it was always Richard and me, the main team, and then our girls. We took great care of our connection as friends and lovers, and enjoyed the tremendous benefits of true partnership. We did this by prioritizing our relationship before the kids' needs. While it is popular to say that "the kids come first," in my opinion, that structure is very damaging to the core relationship and family unit. The best thing you can do for your children is to let them see and feel the love and respect you have for each other, which stands before everything else.

Common sense tells us that the ship will sink without maintenance, and a relationship is the same way. In a marriage, or any committed relationship, it takes practice to nourish an intimate connection after you have children. Set your intention to create the best relationship you can, and to foster friendship in your partnership. Do this by making time for each other every day, without the kids present or the television in the background. Early risers, our best time together was in the wee hours of the morning when we had our coffee, meditated, and talked. That was our ritual. Not only were the strategies in the Don't Sweat series born out of many of our early morning conversations, but also our connection burned brightly for twenty-five years.

The other thing we did was to always have "date" night. For years, we dedicated time each week just for us. We would go horseback riding and take a picnic and hike. Sometimes it was dinner and a movie. When the grandparents were available to babysit, we slipped away for an occasional weekend. We had lunch together several times a week, and we ran and exercised together when we could. We continued to find new ways of enjoying time together and new interests to share.

Make sure your partner is first on your list, and that their needs are not last—and that this is reciprocated back to you. Maintaining a vital connection is critical to the longevity of your union, and ultimately, a thriving family unit. The love that you have for each other is the greatest gift you can give your children.

20

GRATITUDE IS A FAMILY PRACTICE, AND BEGINS WITH YOU

✻ If you want your children to have a positive outlook and see their circumstances with optimism, a good place to start is with your own gratitude. Gratitude is like a sunflower, with you being the center with all the seeds. Some days it's easier to have it than others, but recognizing what is good and positive in our lives can always start small and grow bigger. As you practice living in appreciation, it will become as natural to you as breathing. You will discover that true abundance is not material and does not depend on having more. Abundance comes from wanting what you already have. In your home, an attitude of thankfulness begins with you; it really is contagious.

Learning to place your attention on appreciation is a practice that can change the way you experience your life. A good place to start is when you wake up in the quiet time of the early morning. Say a prayer or meditation of thanks. For instance, my prayer goes something like this: "Divine Love, thank you for my good health; the blessings of my children, grandchildren; and the health of my parents." I continue into my circle of family and friends, and then spend some time being thankful for the joyous moments and unexpected opportunities in my life, be they personal or professional. I acknowledge my gratitude for having nutritious food to eat and a wonderful home to live in. The point is, I try to notice the people and the good things about my life, right from the start of my day.

Sometimes our lives take a hard turn. We may be facing a professional transition, a rough patch in our marriage, or with our kids. Whatever the circumstance, try to bring your attention to small things to be grateful for that may have become invisible to you or otherwise taken for granted. My friend Julia is ending her marriage of many years. It is a time of financial and emotional turbulence; her husband has left her for the perennial "other woman," in this case, her best friend. Julia has children, and her priority has been to keep her head above water and not fall into a depression. Amidst her pain, she keeps a gratitude journal. She has had two very difficult years, but she continues to focus on the things that she is grateful for—her son and daughter, her supportive family and friends, the strength and resiliency she didn't know she had. When you focus on the positive, the negative things are still there, but the sting to your heart is softened. Often, you will find that working out solutions to your problems becomes easier because your heart remains open to possibility.

As a family, we can teach our kids to practice gratitude by making it a ritual at family dinners or at bedtime. Ask them questions: What are three good things that happened to you today? Ask them what they wish they could change about their day. What kindness or acts of character did they express today? Did they do anything to make another person's day better? Engage them in conversation while remembering that the opportunity to reflect helps them to notice the good stuff—what went well—and also gives them the opportunity to share what was hard for them. Maturity is about recognizing that life embraces both. True gratitude is, above all else, about finding contentment when we can love all of life and embrace all things as they are. It's important to acknowledge both good and bad, but always end with a focus on the positive and being appreciative. Wanting what we have and feeling gratitude is the key that brings harmony and true abundance into our lives.

21

ASK THE QUESTION:
WHY DO WE DO IT THIS WAY?

✾ If there is one thing I would value highest in raising children, it is showing up consciously in your parenting. Today's empowered parent chooses to lead their home in a purposeful, practical, and loving manner. Conscious parenting is really about self-awareness; the more self-aware you are, the better you can set your family's conditions and boundaries. This includes deciding what family traditions and rituals you desire to pass down, and why they make sense to you now. Most important, through your mindfulness, you can break any chains of negative and abusive behavior that have been passed down through your relatives. We tend to mythologize the idea of the "perfect" American family, but in truth, every family has some pattern of dysfunction. Moreover, not everyone realizes that they have the power to make change happen for future generations. While much of what you learned from your family you will pass down to your children—and hopefully it will be the good stuff—it doesn't mean that you have to do all the same things in the same way as your parents did them. Sometimes you need to question why things were done in a certain way.

Here's a humorous example of how traditions can get started and perpetuate until someone asks: Why do we do this, in this way? It's important to evaluate your beliefs and be inquisitive about why you do the things you do. One of my friends tells a story about how she removed the ends of the ham when she cooked it for her holiday dinner. One day her mother-in-law asked her why she removed the ends of the ham. She responded, "Well, my mom always removed the ends from the ham when she cooked it." Then, she asked her mom why she removed the ends of the ham and her mom replied, "Because Grandma did it that way. I suppose it makes it cook better." My friend went to her grandmother and asked why she removed the ends of the ham. Her response? "I removed the ends of the ham so that it would fit into my pan."

Of course, the ways we carry dysfunction through our family lineage are not so funny. To break the chain, I must pause to ask myself: What dysfunctional behaviors do I practice by habits that come from my own subconscious psychological patterning because of my upbringing? Emotional patterns and ways of being are handed down from generation to generation like family heirlooms—and while many may be positive, many can also be oppressive.

You can be grateful for the hundred thousand things your mom did right, and as a mom yourself, you should give her many kudos for the loving care she gave you. However, during those times when you say to yourself, "Oh my God, I sound just like my mother!" and it doesn't feel good, this is where you need to ask the question: In this moment, am I choosing consciously how I want to do things in my home? Is this what I really want for my children?

Unless we question and choose what we really want for our children, we will likely continue to replicate patterns that have been passed down to us and are buried in our subconscious minds. So, as a practice, you may want to look at your personal system of values and evaluate them by making a detailed list. The beauty of this practice is that as you grow and change and become more aware, it's okay for your values to change, too, and reflect your growth.

Then ask yourself the question: What do I really want for my kids, and why? As you do this, think about why you feel the way you do about each value on your list, and question your belief system and how it works for you now. You can decide what you really want for your children, and do things your way. Your own parents did many things right. Pass those along, and let go of the ones that didn't work for you.

TAPPING AWAY YOUR FEARS,
WORRY, AND ANXIETY

There is a lot of conversation by new and more experienced mothers around sleep issues. I don't think any children are entirely free from them, and there is a lot of helpful literature that addresses specific sleep topics. When the night comes, dealing with fear and anxiety isn't easy, whether you are a child or an adult, for that matter, but it is a part of life for all of us and presents us with an opportunity to develop some powerful techniques for our emotional tool belt. I was introduced to one of my favorites tools several years ago when I took our daughter to a therapist for some anxiety issues she was having about test performance. She recommended we look into the Emotional Freedom Techniques commonly known as "tapping." It's really quite simple, and it works. You can literally tap away your fears, worries, and anxiety, and so can your children.

The technique combines the powerful use of suggestion through verbal statements and tapping your body, using two fingers in specific sequences at very specific locations on the body that are known as energetic meridians. (This technique is also known as Chinese acupressure.) These points are meant to stimulate the health and flow of energy through the body, while releasing any blocked energy that gets stored in the body through trauma or negative emotions like worry, fear, anger, or guilt. It is a form of relaxation and clearing that is more sophisticated than most techniques.

I'd like to share an example of how it worked with my good friend Amy's three-year-old. Her little daughter Bella had once slept beautifully through the night but now had a far more active imagination and was afraid to go to sleep at night. Small children don't know that their thoughts are not real, but made up by imagination, and therefore their fears and dreams seem completely real to them. Bella somehow had fixated on a monster-like character that scared her, and when she was tucked into her bed, she was sure this character was going to come and get her. After exhausting various ideas and suggestions over a period of weeks, Amy decided to give "tapping" a try.

While I recommend you research the topic online and consider working with a practitioner, here's how "tapping" worked for Bella. At bedtime, with Bella settling down and in her mommy's arms beside her, Amy began by making statements that acknowledged Bella's fear of going to sleep. She began to speak words of comfort and assertion that the monster would not come back tonight, or ever, as she tapped slowly and rhythmically at her daughter's acupressure points at her wrist and clavicle. Bella tapped, too. "Even though I am afraid of the monster," Amy said in a quiet tone, "and even though I see dark shadows and it scares me, there is no monster hiding there and I am safe." Next, Amy continued to tap gently while speaking in soft, soothing tones and moving through the meridian points again (there are about nine), tapping with two fingers while whispering powerful statements to her daughter, suggesting: "Tonight, I'm going to have a good night's sleep, I love being a big girl, I know I'm safe, I know my mommy is with me, I'm going to happily let sleep find me." The very first night Amy and Bella practiced this technique, Amy was able to leave the room without Bella crying or crawling into her parents' bed in the middle of the night.

A further note on sleep: This is another effective strategy unrelated to the technique of tapping. It is something that helped me immeasurably with babies and sleep. When you put your child to sleep, it's important that they know how to comfort themselves. That means when they go to sleep, they go to sleep on their own. Do not stay with them until they fall asleep. Keep your part of the sleep plan limited to a simple bedtime routine, but always walk out the door while they are awake. The reason for this is that the last thing children remember when they fall asleep is the first thing they want when they wake up. If they wake up in the middle of the night, and you are the last thing they remember—for example, you rocking them or nursing them to sleep—it's you they will want. If it's their blanket, or their stuffed animal, that they comforted themselves to sleep with initially, they will find it and cuddle it, and go back to sleep as they return to their own nighttime routine. Sweet dreams.

23

PERSONAL GROWTH CAN BE FUN!

✿ Personal growth isn't about beating yourself up, it's about celebrating your ability to refine and enhance yourself, and increase your personal development through awareness. A mom's journey of personal growth sometimes takes a backseat to other priorities, but that doesn't mean it can't be fun, effective, and a family experience. Your personal expression can be like the stone skipping across the lake, with your energetic ripple moving far and wide as you do your inner personal growth work. It truly has a positive effect on your family and surrounding community.

There are times with kids that are overwhelming because we are burdened by the magnitude of responsibility. In the past, when I had time to take a respite away from family, I would always take a journal with me. As soon as you step out of your life and you are no longer micromanaging, everything gets blurry in a good way, and only what needs to be focused on will surface.

Personal growth is all about reflecting and noticing the thoughts that simply don't serve my family or me. Past grudges, regrets, anger, resentment, fears, and other emotional baggage only hinder the happiness in my spirit and our home. In essence, it is a spring-cleaning of unhealthy attachments.

As I made this move toward an inner directedness, lighter insights, and healthier thoughts and patterns, my family couldn't help but notice the difference. This gave me the opportunity to share this process with them and encourage them to do the same.

When the self-critic is silenced, personal growth becomes a healthy road toward an improved life. My personal goal has been to pick at least one workshop a year to attend, with a focus on personal enhancement. All the incredible tele-seminars make it easy to do a virtual retreat and have access to our favorite authors and speakers. For some quiet time, take a yoga class or meditate, or get together with some girlfriends to make it social. Encourage each other and offer positive observations about each other while you share your insights through e-mail or in a group setting. It is important that the experience be uplifting and inspiring.

I know a mom who would post her inspirational reading quote for the day, as her personal morning ritual, on her chalkboard in the kitchen, and all the kids would read it during breakfast. (You can imagine the profound impact those words had when they were subliminally taken in with oatmeal spoon to mouth.) Your personal growth can be done as a family activity, too.

In January, you can make it a family ritual to do a vision board by laying out magazines, poster boards, scissors, and glue sticks on the table.

Each of you can sit around your table and create a collage using the pictures and letters you cut and paste to dream about what you would like to create and attract in your life vision for the new year. You can also do a family vision board, and design it specific to a vacation you will be taking or are dreaming up. Or simply just do it for creative leisure and time spent together on a winter day.

This process of fun personal development ensures healthy thinking and lasting change that is built on a base of positivity, not criticism. Being a mom often makes it challenging to take time for personal growth; I've never had a positive insight or come into a new awareness that didn't directly affect my marriage or my children in a positive way. And, when built into fun family and personal activities, the impact a personal growth exercise or activity can have on your life and home is immeasurable. Make it fun—make it count—and teach your kids through your example that nourishing our spirit and doing our inner work makes life a whole lot brighter for everyone.

24

WE CAN'T CUSHION EVERY BLOW, BUT WE CAN SOFTEN THEM

As adults, we know that life isn't fair. We also know that learning how to move through the minor disappointments that happen in childhood helps us to prepare for life's larger adversities. When Tommy doesn't make the team he tries out for, or Sally doesn't get the part in her theater drama, or Jamie receives a B on a test she studied hard for, this is a monumental disappointment. Life itself is a classroom and a playground. As mothers, we can't cushion every blow our kids receive, but we can soften those blows by helping our children to see that we are not defined by the successes or failures we have, as much as by our work ethic, our tenacity, and the efforts we put in to achieve our goals.

When kids receive a blow or disappointment, the most important thing you can do first is to validate their feelings. You can acknowledge the disappointment by saying: "I know it feels really bad to try your best and not get what you want, and right now, it feels like the end of the world to you. I felt the same way when I didn't make my grade or team at your age." Or, "If you tried your best, then maybe this isn't your season.

But if you work harder and give it more time, you will be more seasoned and ready when the time is right."

Your kids know that just because they don't receive the accolade, it doesn't mean failure in your eyes. Show your child that you love her the same, unconditionally, just as you did before, and just as you always will. As one wise friend told her child, "This is one disappointment; in your lifetime, there will be many, just as wonderful things will also happen that you've worked hard for. This is one slice of the pizza. It's happened and it makes you feel sad, but it's not the whole pie."

As adults, we have experienced enough in life to recognize that sometimes you have to lose to win. As my friend author Steve Maraboli says, "Sometimes the greatest messages can be found in the greatest messes." It is often in these times of letdown that there is an unforeseen opportunity to help our kids to see, understand, or emphasize something that might have otherwise gone unnoticed. As you talk about the situation, you can help them see what they may do better or more effectively next time. They may see that other, new possibilities exist—a chance, for instance, for Sally to work on the crew and learn about lighting or set decoration; a chance for Jamie to improve her note-taking skills; and a possibility for Tommy to have more playing time by joining a less competitive team. We can't stop our kids from falling down, but we can be there to help them as they get up.

We live in a world that demands and expects so much of us. Surviving minor setbacks will help our kids learn to move through the real challenges that life throws at us later, with greater grace. Sports can offer many good examples of this. When your children are involved in sports, there will always be a game they wish they had won or a play they wish they had made. But in life, much as in sports, sometimes, regardless of how hard you try, things don't turn out the way you planned. This truth about life isn't something we need to protect our children from. Instead, it is an opportunity to help them release their attachment to an outcome they can't control, and to focus on their personal contribution and on doing their best. Help them to always see the big picture when something doesn't go right, and the possibility that something better will be right around the corner.

25

INSTEAD OF ASKING
WHAT'S WRONG, ASK WHAT'S RIGHT

Most of us don't need much help with venting our frustrations about life, but a good dose of what's right can help shift your kids from a low mood into laughter. It can also show them that there's always a second perspective.

My girlfriend Dana picked up her eight-year-old son, Will, from school the other day. She watched him walk slowly toward the car, open the door, and then slump down into his seat. He barely grunted "hello" to her. She did what any concerned parent would do and asked: "Hey, honey, what's wrong?" Will's response was: "I don't know, I just had a bad day." Dana had a brilliant reply. She said: "Okay, if you can't tell me what's wrong, then tell me what's right!" She began to coax him out of his bad mood by asking: "Did you have a good snack at snack time?" (She knew he did, because she had packed it earlier that morning.) "Tell me about something funny that happened today. How are your classroom rabbits doing? After the other day, when that girl in your class forgot to lock the cage after she cleaned it, are they doing another runaway bunny routine? What else?" Before long, she and Will were laughing and making a game out of "What's right with your day." His mood lifted, and when they got home, he ran out the door to play, forgetting all about his bad day.

"What's right with your day?" helps all of us remember that there is always a bright side. As a culture, we tend to focus on the negative (Murphy's Law: Everything that can go wrong, will go wrong!), while the good things tend to go unnoticed. I know this for a fact—there was a time when, as I spoke in the mornings with my girlfriends, we'd spend the first few minutes of most conversations "venting" to one another about the little irritations of our day—the slights, the inconveniences, the tedium of our routines, and the variability of our relationships with our families. The good things sometimes got introduced almost as an afterthought. Life feels really good when we are in a high mood, and not so good when we are low. A low mood will spiral even lower when we place our attention only on the negative things that happen in our lives. More important, that's exactly what we are facilitating when we ask our kids, "What's wrong?" It's far easier to shift out of a low mood when we focus our attention on the positive things in our day, small as they may be.

Being present to what's right in your life will help you and your children swing into a higher mood and back onto a happier track. It is in this attitude of gratitude that our children can get out of their slumps and find their smiles again. And we all know that nothing is more uplifting than a smile from our children. Try it, the next time you are in this situation with your child. Simply ask, "What's right?" Teach him or her to understand that you don't have to have a good day, but there is always a different way of seeing it.

26

JUST SIT WITH IT

How many times have your kids tested your patience by slumping onto the couch as if to say, "Mom! I'm bored!"? And, if you are anything like me, you would think to yourself with rueful envy, *If only I could be so lucky*! If your first reaction to their comment is panic that they're not stimulated enough, or that something is wrong, think again. Maybe nothing is amiss at all. Boredom isn't always a bad thing. It's nothing more than a lack of engagement in the opportunity presented at that moment. Sometimes, boredom is just what a kid needs.

After delivering Jasmine, I went to my doctor for my first checkup. The baby was tucked away at home with Richard, and I remember just relishing the time to be alone. I sat in the waiting room for about half an hour, not even tempted to pick up a magazine. I hadn't had a moment to myself since giving birth four weeks before. Previously, I would have been impatient at waiting so long for the doctor to see me; now, I was enjoying the time I spent just sitting there with nothing to do. I remember telling myself I didn't think I would ever be "bored" again. And, do you know what? Twenty-two years later, I can honestly say I haven't been.

Have you ever heard a three-year-old say they are bored? There is no such thing for such a child. Little ones are too immersed in creatively exploring their world.

It's only as our children get older that they become aware of the idea that being present is not enough. We don't have to look far to see where that idea comes from; our own busy lives model it for them. We schedule our kids as we schedule our own days—packed full. And so when the kids whine that they have nothing to do, it is usually an indication of over-stimulation and a lack of presence. Like the adults around them, they have become addicted to the excitement of the next best thing to do. As Richard would say, we've become dangerously close to becoming "human doings" rather than "human beings." Let us learn to simply be.

The next time your kids complain about not having something to do, realize that this is not a problem you really need to solve. It is actually an opportunity to embrace downtime. Instead of suggesting ten things they can get busy with, suggest that they just sit with it and see what comes up for them. In these moments, there are real opportunities—for appreciation, creativity, and reflection—that are otherwise missed. Let them learn to savor the stillness of the empty spaces. And, even though I'm not sure I've ever heard a mom say she's bored, I suggest that, should you find yourself so lucky, you take the time to just sit with it, too. Crack a smile and say to your child: "I've got a good idea. Let's just sit here and be bored for a while together."

27

WHOSE DREAM IS THIS, ANYWAY?

We bring our children into the world, but they don't really belong to us like possessions. It's a cliché, but a true one, that many parents live vicariously through their kids. As their mom, we are there to help them discover their dreams, assist them in becoming who they are, and also enjoy the process of their development. Many times, however, it's the parents who hold the vision for their child, and although with good intent, they push them too hard to achieve higher levels of performance. As any young person displays talent and progresses in competition and rank, it's important for you to ask yourself: *Whose dream is this, anyway? Is it my dream for you, or yours?*

When you see beauty-pageant moms parading around their tiara-wearing toddlers and biting their nails, you know it's the mom who finds this world intriguing. While there may be a rare child who gels with this lifestyle and is a natural performer at this age, it's usually these pageant moms who are the impetus for it, hoping that these little girls will turn into something that was unfulfilled in them.

We've also all heard of the stage mother who pushes a child to excel, whether it is on the stage, a dance floor, an ice rink, a tennis court, or anywhere else. We can't help but remember the Gypsy Rose Lees of the world, or how Andre Agassi's dad put a racket into his son's hand in early childhood and drilled the child into exhaustion and pain. Agassi came to eventually hate tennis in spite of the many millions he made, a mixed blessing that he readily acknowledges. So, yes, it's complicated. Sometimes a parent's dream reflects a pragmatic opportunity for the child to have a better life materially than the one they were born into. Oftentimes, however, parents push their kids simply to enjoy the reflected glory. When the child doesn't feel the passion, a dream can become a nightmare.

There are children who burn brightly with ambition and the talent to match. I know a family that is supporting a child for the right reasons. Sarah and Mike's fifteen-year-old daughter loves performing in community theater and wants more than anything else to try her luck in Hollywood. They are in a financial position and have the career flexibility to relocate the family and support their daughter's dream. In this instance, there is no question of who is dreaming the dream. Both parents have performance backgrounds, so they understand their daughter's passion; moreover, they have a realistic view which has been purposefully conveyed to her about how difficult it is to create a viable career as an actress. In these circumstances with this family, all the dominos lined up happily, and parents and child chose their dream together, living life adventurously.

We can do no more as parents than to support our children in nourishing their hopes and aspirations. But the dream has to be theirs. Life is not about do-overs when it comes to your unresolved issues. You may have wanted to be a competitive athlete or performer or musician yourself, but it didn't work out for you. That doesn't mean you get another chance at it because there's a genetic match. It's easy to forget that our children are merely in our care, and that they are separate individuals. If you are pushing your child, there will come a day when they just don't have the juice necessary to perform any longer because it is not their passion, but yours. There is a reasonable chance that they will not forgive you for stealing their soul, and a part of their childhood, so is it worth the risk? I don't think so.

By asking the question for your kids: *Whose dream is this anyway?*, you will avoid living vicariously, and perhaps will realize that you still have dreams of your own.

28

IT'S NOT ABOUT HOW OLD YOU ARE

❁ I was recently inspired by a comment I read that said, "I don't think people should be allowed to have children if they are under the age of twenty-five." There are a lot reasons why it would be nice if there were some sort of threshold for women to meet before deciding to have a child. It would be nice if all women had a chance to complete their educations; to live independently in the world; to take parenting classes; and had some money in the bank . . . and my list could go on. But, I don't believe age is one of those prerequisites that create good moms.

Sure, it might be easier if every baby came into the world at just the right time for its parents—if there is ever a truly "right" time. There are probably better times than others for all of us when taking into consideration the financial responsibilities attached to motherhood. But whatever their age, young mothers and older mothers pay very different, but equally significant, individual prices for choosing motherhood. Motherhood pitches you right out of every single thing you anticipated your life to be, and into something profoundly unexpected.

The young mother may not have had enough time on her own to know herself first as the woman she is; she may not yet have had the time and freedom to establish her independent identity. And the older mother, well, she lacks the same youthful stamina she once had, which makes it harder on her physically to rise to the many challenges of parenting—especially chasing after young children, who have boundless energy. Yet I have seen both young and more mature moms manage just fine. That is because the one quality good moms share is the ability to sense and nurture her child's needs, while nature takes care of the rest. All things considered, in a perfect world, it might be true that wisdom comes with age, but delight in new experiences has traditionally been seen as the province of youth. Both are essential ingredients of good parenting.

My daughter Jasmine became pregnant while taking birth control. She was nineteen years old and in a committed relationship. Jazz fell within the 3 percent of women who impregnate while on the Pill. She wasn't ready for this any more than she was ready to lose her father at the age of seventeen. Sometimes, life just happens.

I was amazed at how Jazz cared for her body during pregnancy. Quite honestly, I was five years older than she and in a settled and loving marriage when I became pregnant. She did a better job in gestation at her tender age than I did. I have marveled at what a wonderful mother she is and how she cares for her young son with attentive and natural ease. He is her top priority, and she shows him the same love that I have always shown her, even while she juggles his needs with school. She has made multiple sacrifices to create this new life for herself and her son.

She has grown up faster than her peers. Maturity holds layers of meaning to her that are lost on them. Would she like to have had carefree twenties? Yes. Would she have liked to be an ordinary college coed, making decisions that are no more complicated than course selection? Yes. But would she choose to exchange the life she has for a life without her son? Never.

We have yet to discover a science for raising our children. While there are plenty of experts and dozens of philosophies out there, there seems to be no rhyme or reason that explains how a child brought up by a single mother under stressful circumstances could grow up to be president of the United States, while a child raised in a solid, comfortable middle-class home could turn out to be the mastermind of a giant Ponzi scheme and a convicted felon. There is no true way or age that defines what it means to be a good mother.

No matter what your age, the greatest gift you can give your child is your intention to give him or her the best home you can with what you have. The material stuff? That's the small stuff. The real stuff, the stuff that matters, is what comes from your heart. Love is ageless and bottomless. It's not about how old you are! Love is the most important ingredient when being a mom, at any age.

29

WAITING FOR A TEACHING MOMENT

Timing is everything, especially when it comes to breaking through the barriers of communication with our children. It's important to stay abreast of what's going on with them, behind the scenes, so that you can find the right teaching moment to talk together. This requires some tact, along with strategic planning, on your part. At times, you have to keep your ears open and your mouth shut. And because there is a lot going on with your kids that they won't tell you, a cautious, observing silence is sometimes your most effective asset. Storing away information and waiting for the right moment to talk about an issue is as important as anything else you can do.

A situation that came to my attention recently reinforced this point. I was listening to two mothers talk about their teenagers. Their daughters, Briana and Dena, are best friends. The girls often go out together and spend the night at each other's houses. One of the women said to the other, "I thought you should know that the girls went to a party the other night when you were out of town. I'm not sure that Dena told you about it." I watched the woman's reaction as her jaw clenched tightly and her brow creased. She said, shaking her head, "Well, that's a totally different story than Dena told me. I'm going to get her when she walks through that door today. I hate it when she lies to me like this."

What troubles me about this mom's reaction is that, rather than teaching Dena she needs to tell her the truth, it appears that she is more interested in attacking her daughter. So an issue about respecting her parent's rules will turn into an issue around control. This is classic dysfunction: Dena withholds information from her mother as in "I'm not going to tell you what I'm doing because you'll say no." Rather than looking to understand that there may be a reason why her daughter is lying, by responding from a reactive and hot-tempered position, the girl's mother is almost willfully challenging the daughter to lie again. I also suspect that, as the saying goes, "Apples don't fall far from the tree," and Dena is probably as stubborn as her mom; jumping on her daughter the minute she walks through the door is not going to ease the problem. A more fruitful approach would be to let the incident go—this time—but next time that Dena mentions that she's spending the night at her friend's house, the mother should remind Dena that she has to follow her rules, even when she's away from home, reminding her, that if it turns out that the evening is not as Dena described it, she will find out, and there will be consequences.

Often, our kids don't tell us what's really going on because they know very well the kinds of reactions they will receive from us. But I would argue that the best thing this mom can do would be to wait and to store this information away instead for the next time. She can give Dena the opportunity to tell her what she will be doing, and catch her in the act if her daughter lies to her. Behind the lying, there is a conversation that needs to happen between mother and daughter where there is a teaching moment.

Another mom I know keeps her ears open in the car during car pool. She will play music and turn the front speakers off and the back speakers on, so she can listen to what the kids are saying. The snippets of information she gathers allow her to stay in tune with what they are really into, because the children completely forget she's in the car. Now, some people might think of this as eavesdropping, and truthfully, it is, but as a mom, you can think of it as intelligence gathering, to know where your conversation needs to go for the next teaching moment.

The teaching moment occurs when your son or daughter says something that gives you a good lead. For example, if you were listening to the boys in your car talking disrespectfully about a group of girls, you would want to wait for the right opportunity to discuss what it means to have respect for the opposite sex.

The point here is to keep your eyes and ears open and wait for the right moment to speak about a particular topic. Your words will have far greater impact when you hold on to your information and wait for the teaching moment. Then, when your kid opens the door, you can walk right on in.

30

POWERED WITH YOUR PASSION

The times I remember being most happy in motherhood are those when I held my family close but also nourished my own spirit by doing something for me. True nourishment of my spirit didn't have to do with having the occasional spa day, ladies lunch, or date night with Richard (although these things were important to balance, too). Rather, I felt most nourished when I was involved in a worthwhile project that satisfied my individual sense of self-expression. I did this through art, writing, and charitable work.

After years of running my own graphic design business and, later, working as a marketing telecommunications consultant, once the girls came along, I stayed home with them for the most part and managed our household and organized our lives. Structure is not a quality that is natural to me, yet it feels very necessary to family life. But I noticed pretty quickly that, much as I loved my life, routine could become pretty stultifying. I was my happiest self when I could change it up and add an art project, a home remodeling project, board work, training for a marathon to help find a cure for leukemia, fund-raising for a charity, or participating in a business venture—even though my first priority was always family. I knew I needed outside interests to inspire and rejuvenate me.

As moms, we need to fill our own well so that everyone else in our family has plenty to drink. Family life pulls at our energy levels, and suppressing our passion is exhausting, too. When we don't sustain ourselves, the well goes dry. Sustaining ourselves has to do with tapping into the divine flow around us and powering that force with passion—whatever it is you love to do, do more of that.

While it certainly is our most important work, the truth is we can become over-identified in our role as a mother. It's also important to express ourselves personally outside the framework of raising kids. We may do that through education, in an art or cooking class, for instance, or in any number of activities and hobbies that gratify your soul. These things feed our enthusiasm for the rest of our activities that we have to do and that may not be all that fun. Some of us find this extra-family satisfaction through careers and paid work; others find it through service and volunteerism. All of us thirst for it.

Dana Hilmer is a blogger, writer, and mother of three. She wrote in her anthology, *Blindsided by a Diaper,* that understanding that transitioning from a full-time career to "Mom" meant she had to be creative in how she balanced her work life with changing diapers and successive pregnancies. She said: "It's too easy to lose your sense of self in caring for your family." Her books and radio show add to her family life because it gives her a creative outlet she is truly passionate about, not to mention extra income.

If your life lacks exuberance and joy, take some time to first sit with your intuition and feelings. Then, make a bucket list as you attempt to answer these questions: If you were not limited by time or money, what would you be doing as an authentic expression of your spirit? What are the things that bring a rush of joy and excitement to you, that make you smile just to think of them? If there were no obstacles stopping you, how would you like to spend some time each day? What are you putting on hold in your life? These don't have to be grand plans; they can be small things like arranging flowers, gardening or painting, performing in community theater, or participating in a social action project. Review your list and decide on one of those things that you could devote a couple of hours to each day . . . and then just do it!

These days, I have to smile, because now that my girls are grown, my time management issues continue to be spent creating balance—ironically in reverse! I have many passionate interests and a full-time career. The balance now comes in taking time off of work to be with my family. I spend time with Kenna, going to Bikram yoga class together, and while Jazz attends school I take care of my grandson, Caden. We call them "Nana Mondays." For the first year of his life, even while I was finishing and on tour for my book *Heartbroken Open*, I blocked out every Monday to be with him. I have to smile at how life changes order. I have lived both sides and know that, either way, having one without the other is not at all fulfilling.

When we lose our sense of self, we starve our true nature. We feed ourselves when we do something out of the ordinary or explore an outside interest. We refuel our energy and bring that sense of wonder back into our life, which penetrates the rest of our activities with a new sense of exuberance. Whether our adventures take us back to familiar but nearly forgotten territory, or launch us onto fertile new ground, when we are passionately engaged with life we have so much more to give to those who depend on us to shape theirs. Self-expression will invigorate you. When your life is powered with passion, the rewards to your spirit will be astounding.

31

MOTHER KNOWS BEST

There are a lot of things to worry about while raising our families. I don't have to review them—you know what I mean. As we go through the journey of motherhood, we have to develop a filter that helps us determine which concerns really require us to take action and which ones will pass on their own. While it's always helpful to have the advice, opinions, and constructive advice of more experienced family and friends, it's important to find your own answers as to the way you will raise your family. Your family and friends can offer valuable input, but it is ultimately up to you to decide on the best route for your child.

Our challenges are often aggrandized by our fears. Many of our concerns initially may seem like huge obstacles to tackle and overcome. That is because we often overthink what the long-range meaning or consequences of a situation might be, and truth is, we don't really know. If, as a strategy, you realize you don't know what the future holds, you become less reactive to your worries and fears, and instead more responsive to the issue or problem at hand. This allows you to make your decisions from calm resolve instead of frenetically being overwhelmed. In fact, most of your worries can be solved by making a series of small changes in order to negotiate a new path.

My friend Marla called one day to ask my advice, mom to mom. She is the mother of three daughters, all stair-stepping in age about two years apart. Each of them has a cherub face framed by flowing ringlet curls. They are sweet and kind girls, and together are a lovely family. Marla explained that some visiting family members had commented judgmentally about the girls and their weight. Apparently, the grandparents were concerned that Marla's oldest daughter, only twelve, bordered on "obesity." Marla asked me if I thought she should put Lacey on a diet.

As her friend, I could see Marla was reacting to her fear about what might be in store for Lacey, suddenly concerned about every issue that might be ahead for the child, from diabetes to bullying. Knowing she was completely caught up in her worries and fear, I said: "Hey, let's take a deep breath here and talk about this." I began to ask her questions as we discussed the family's meal plan and looked at ideas to improve it. We spoke about limiting the amount of carbohydrates they consume, and about making small changes, such as avoiding eating pasta for the evening meal and adding more white meat chicken, fish, and vegetables. We also talked about introducing more aerobic activities into their day, such as sports or dance class. I encouraged Marla to consult with Lacey's pediatrician and maybe have her thyroid tested. Most important, I suggested she speak with her girls, but in such a way that would not put stress on the way they currently feel about their bodies and their weight.

Finally, I pointed out to Marla that her girls all share similar body types, and that that was certainly based on their genetics. Therefore, while making these small changes would enhance their physical health and lifestyle, they would unlikely see significant changes in their appearance right away. Before we got off the phone, I asked Marla: "Hey, out of curiosity, were you concerned with the girls' weight before your family made these critical comments?" She answered: "No, not really. I know my kids aren't typical California beach girls, but they seem comfortable in their bodies, and they are healthy. I think that as they age, their shapes will be curvy, though they will slim out more in time as they grow into their bodies." I replied: "You are their mother, and you know what's best for them. I think you're right."

Often, our worries and concerns are bigger enemies than the issue we face. Marla could easily have become fearful after her family raised the weight issue. It was very wise for her not to react, but instead to reach out for support and encouragement from a trusted friend. She then responded to the concerns of her family by implementing small lifestyle changes and by speaking to her daughters about their health in uncritical terms.

I have learned that what you are worried about now won't be what you are concerned with two years from now. Life has its own way of replacing the concern you just worked through with a shiny new one.

When you act from fear, you can lose sight of the long-range goal, which is to move in a new direction as painlessly as possible to achieve the desired end result. If we react rather than respond, our fears can immobilize us and keep us from preparing a plan of action.

It may very well take a village to raise a child, but no one knows your kids quite the same way as you do. As long as you respond to most issues and problems in baby steps, none of them will be completely overwhelming. There are few problems that are truly insurmountable, and mother (almost) always knows best.

32

A NEW PARADIGM FOR
SEPARATED PARENTS

With more than 50 percent of marriages ending in divorce, you are not alone if your marriage or your relationship doesn't work out. More important, if you manage your personal healing and hold the intention that you will do everything possible to prioritize the best interests of your kids, you don't have to feel like you failed. How you proceed will minimize the emotional turbulence your kids experience. When things don't work out between Mom and Dad, it doesn't mean that everything has to fall apart for them, especially in families where parents share the same concerns, put a value on family life, and really do want what's best for their children. If this is true, it can't just be lip service; it requires that no matter what emotional wounds you carry or what legal issues may still be pending between you, you and your ex are committed to finding your way to a loving—or at least functional—friendship that strengthens the partnership you have as co-parents.

I've seen couples who have come to the end of their marriage or committed partnership, and who are modeling a truly amicable new arrangement where Mom and Dad stay friends and parental partners. One key thing that these couples do immediately after their separation is they stop playing the "blame game." Both acknowledge and take responsibility for their part in the breakup of their relationship. It has been proven that parents who blame each other in front of the children create an environment of alienation that critically damages the children's ability to flourish after a divorce. Those parents who can eventually look each other in the eyes, and appreciate the good things and times they had together as a couple—and as a family—despite the fact that today they choose to live separately, are better able to sustain a co-parenting friendship. Friendship and mutual respect help them to maintain a united approach for their kids.

Of course, some relationships end badly—in fact, very badly. Forgiveness may follow, or maybe it won't. Often, forgiveness takes years, years you don't have while your children are moving through their own growing years. They need you to be present emotionally and physically, and they need that other parent to do the same. So the best approach you can take is to stop playing the role of victim. While you may feel that you upheld your end of the marriage agreement in your heart and mind, you have to put aside the fact that your partner, for any variety of reasons, could not sustain his feelings or commitment in the same ways. Forgiveness is imperative to moving forward.

As you are able to heal your differences and honor the truth and essence of the other person for who they are and not who you wish they were, you are moving the relationship to a better, more supportive place.

From this place of forgiveness, you allow your relationship to transcend the boundaries of the original contract of marriage and move into a new form of partnership, where family and the desire for what's best for the kids is the glue that bonds you together. The emotional and intimate personal issues between you cease to exist, and can no longer hurt you.

The couples I know who have forged a new paradigm in the wake of their divorce or separation often "nest" with their children when they have custody in a central location where the kids reside full time, while making other living arrangements for themselves during noncustodial periods. This is complicated, and can only work with two emotionally stable parents. If one is snooping around or jealous, it would not be the best of situations to share space. On the other hand, if you both are amicable and prioritize money savings, this may mean renting a space elsewhere, or even sharing a separate apartment with your ex. These arrangements go a long way toward stabilizing the kids' lives by minimizing their level of disruption during the week.

Living in Northern California as I do, I am accustomed to hearing about all manner and forms of alternative living. But it truly amazed me that when Karen met Ted, who was also divorced with children of his own, that he and Karen and her ex, Brandon, were all able to form a friendship, and eventually also included Ted's ex. This relationship extended to joint family vacations and shared holidays. It takes some very secure well-intentioned individuals to choose to embrace this new paradigm for family where everyone participates as an extended family unit. Under this arrangement, the kids have thrived. The scars of those unhappy years of argument and anger that preceded the divorce, and then the divorce itself, seem nonexistent. Would they wish their parents to still be together? Probably, but possibly they are better off witnessing the fact that two people can find love elsewhere while renewing and reframing an affectionate friendship that once existed, but somehow got lost in the unhappiness of the marriage.

It's important to remember that after a divorce or breakup, it's no longer about the drama between you and your ex. It's about the fact that you both love your kids equally and so greatly that you can make peace with each other. If you can truly appreciate the gifts of these children that came from the love you once shared, then you can choose to make the best of your situation by creating a new paradigm that includes a co-parental partnership and lifelong respect.

33

DATING AND THE SINGLE MOM

I used to shake my head when I thought about how difficult it would be to be a single mom, with all the things that need to get done in a day! Managing your home, your kids, and your personal life while pretending that there's time to manage even one of these areas. A single mom has all the responsibilities of every other mom, but doesn't have the backup support at home of a partner. She falls into bed at night alone, with no one present to listen to her or to have an adult conversation with.

Most single moms I know need time to feel ready for romantic companionship. The reasons may be emotional, or logistical, or both. Each of us—and I am one of you—feels fragile. The loss of a partner, whatever the circumstances, has utterly changed the trajectory of how we expected our lives to go. Healing takes time. Stepping into a new vision of yourself as unattached and sexually attractive takes time. Until you became a single parent, you lived much of your life as a woman first, separate from being a mom, so when you are ready, you deserve some time to be that woman again.

You don't get much time away, so when you do begin to date, make sure your primary goal is to have fun. Engage in the moment, and don't spend this time feeling guilty that you are not with your children. I'm sure you've made good arrangements for their care while you are away for a few short hours. It's natural for you to be searching for romance and physical companionship. Allow yourself the treat of an evening out, to dress nicely, feel good and attractive, be admired, and be forward-looking again. After a few shaky starts, it really does get easier.

We've talked about why it's important for you to date. Now, I'm not trying to scare you, but dating comes with some risk. Here are some tips to keep in mind and keep you and your family safe as you date:

- Ask your date a lot of questions and get to know him well. My friend Maryanne Comaroto, who was a single mom herself for many years, writes an excellent book for women getting out there again, and addresses the questions that you should ask your date in her book *Hindsight: What You Need to Know Before You Drop Your Drawers.*
- Go with the intention to have great conversation and enjoy an evening out. Try not to head-trip about what the relationship means, and remember the strategy: "You'll know when you know." Have fun!

- Meet your date at a place away from your home until you know him and have dated him for several months. Don't let him know your exact address and where you live.
- If you become involved in online dating, never give out your personal e-mail address or telephone number until you feel completely at ease.
- When it comes to introducing a new person into your home, be cautious. As much as you may like him, if you haven't met him through friends or known him in your past, you can't assume that this person is safe around your kids. There is no room for error here when it comes to protecting your children.
- You must really get to know this person and his friends and family before you introduce him to yours. This will give you more information about that person, another way of seeing him in a different context. His friends will tell you a great deal more about his character, choices, and behavior than your dates will. And when you do introduce him to your friends and family, listen to their opinions and observations. They may be seeing something your smitten eyes may not.

Every day a single mom wakes up, she faces a marathon. On the rare occasion when you step out to take care of yourself and your personal needs, you won't carry the resentment and martyrdom of sacrifice that many women feel when they don't date or take time for themselves. Date safely and wisely, and most important, have fun! You deserve it.

34

LEARNING TO SAY "NO!"
SO YOU HAVE TIME TO SAY "YES!"

You probably know her—that "super mom" who spins her wheels all day long, leaving herself frazzled and exhausted. When your intentions are good, and you're capable and competent, it's easy to take on the jobs that will enhance the quality of your kids' education. Would you please run the school's book fair? No problem! Be a grade-level rep on the PTA? Sure! How about organizing the team barbecue after soccer season ends? Okay, I'm on it! And you? You're a serious candidate for burnout. Learning the art of saying "No, thank you, I have too much on my plate right now" will clear your calendar so you can participate fully in the activities that you really want to say "yes" to.

When you enroll your kids in elementary school, you begin to realize that there exists a parallel universe of volunteer work at their schools, and within every sport and activity they participate in. Schools have limited resources, and rely on their parent volunteers to fill in the gaps so that kids have access to extra sports; music and art programs; and computers and books and electronic media that enrich their educations.

Knowing that the volunteer food chain is inexhaustible will help you choose wisely as to where your time can be best spent. Before you say "yes," think about taking on roles that may allow you to use your skills (marketing, writing, financial, and fund-raising, for instance). Also, consider responsibilities that build new skills, including computer skills you may need if you've taken time off to raise your family and decide later to return to the workforce. Also, remember that your work as a volunteer is necessary for getting needed tasks done, but it should be fun, too. You are, after all, a v-o-l-u-n-t-e-e-r. And where you can, work alongside moms you enjoy or would like to get to know. There is no reason why your committee assignment should not be social, too. One woman I know met the woman who would become her closest friend when she agreed to cochair an auction for a new school playground.

In order to implement this strategy, you really have to know when enough is enough and be honest with yourself about how much time you reasonably have to offer. Once you have taken on a leadership role in one school or program, it may be time to turn down other requests or even resign from some of your other obligations. When we overcommit, then most of our free daytime and many evenings and weekends are spent away from our families while we attend board and committee meetings. You want to do your part, of course—but you don't want to do it all.

When you know what your personal threshold is, and you can balance your commitments and still have the time you need at home, then you can really look forward to both. There are many people-pleasers who take on leadership roles because they are afraid to disappoint others, or who don't know how to say, "No, I can't commit to that right now." Or, "I'm sorry, but I chaired that committee last year. It's time for someone else to step up this year." When we are stretched too thin, we feel resentful and abused, rather than satisfied and happy.

My advice to you is to be clear about your priorities in advance and budget out your time. The more children you have in different schools, the more you will have to learn how to say "no" sometimes, because you are already saying "yes" to being the scout leader for Jack, the girls' softball coach for Janie, or helping out at Scott's school library once a week. When you can learn to say "no" without guilt, you will do a much better job doing the things for your family and community you care about most. And you will do so without resentment. You will be more present, energetic, and empowered by the things you've selected to do. And you will find the joy that comes from contributing positively to that which enriches your children's lives, and those of other children in your community.

35

NO MORE BULLYING!

We hear a lot about bullying in the media today, and each story sounds like a sad incident about someone else and having little to do with you until it's your child who's been bullied. Because one in four of all children between the ages of eight and sixteen report that they have been bullied themselves, this is a topic that should hit home for all of us. I am including some strategies to put in place so that you can help your child cope with the situation and feel better.

This may sound somewhat surprising, but it's helpful for your child to understand bullying behavior and where it comes from. This is because it's difficult to access compassion for someone who has caused you to suffer. But allowing your child to understand that the bully is someone who is also hurting because he or she has been bullied themselves will enable your child to take some of the power back. The fact that bullies learned this behavior from feeling powerless themselves makes them less of a monster and more human, on the same playing field.

At the end of his inspirational memoir *Way of the Peaceful Warrior,*

Dan Millman writes a beautiful tale of a bully and his victim becoming friends. Research shows that nearly all bullies have been bullied themselves by a parent, an older sibling, or classmates, and those that hurt others are often the ones hurting most inside. While understanding this won't make a bully go away or excuse his unacceptable behavior, it's good for children to see that bullying makes victims out of everyone.

There are many types of bullying and, because of this, the way you and your child respond will depend on the situation. Most often, children are targeted by virtue of their appearance or social status. Bullying behavior includes hazing and taunting in the halls and cafeterias by another classmate, inappropriate and degrading remarks made by a teacher or coach, bullying on sports fields from teammates, and cyber and social media harassment. By the time your son or daughter comes to you in frustration, chances are a pattern of abuse has been established, and it's not an isolated incident of "kids being kids." Your first course of action should be to listen intently to her feelings and her story, and then to assess the situation. Here are some tips to follow that will help an empowered parent become proactive and help put an end to the cruelty of bullying:

- Report acts of bullying. Enlist the assistance of the school administration and, if appropriate, the local police. Bullying should not go unreported, because the emotional effects on your child are serious. We have learned from school tragedy after school tragedy that children who turn guns on other children, or take their own lives, have themselves been bullied. It's true that kids learn early that being considered a tattletale or "rat" isn't the kind of attention they want either, but standing up to do the right thing is the greatest lesson one can learn at any age. You're not just standing up for him, but for yourself and for all the others that this person will hurt in the future if you withhold and don't say anything. The truth is that this is the only way to ensure that the bullying can stop and the bully may get the help he needs. A young bully who feels a source of power and gets addicted to it can turn into a criminal later in life.

- In cyber-bullying, removing your child from the social media arena will give him or her a low profile for a while.

- Address your child's humiliation at being a target. Affirm to her that she does not deserve this kind of attention, and that it is not a reflection of anything she has done wrong. If need be, explore social opportunities for your child outside his or her school.

- Keep the lines of communication open and keep your child talking to you. As he allows his feelings of anger and hurt to surface, he won't internalize being a victim. Consider professional counseling—experts can not only provide a safe environment for your child of any age to unload his or her feelings, but can also work with your child to change behaviors that may leave them vulnerable, or learn how to stand up for themselves effectively without resorting to violence.

- Ask your school to introduce a program for peer counseling and conflict mediation. Be proactive and bring nonprofit groups in to speak and present anti-bullying workshops to empower parents and children.

- Look for a support group. There is online support available for victims of bullying.

Bullying is big stuff, and is agonizing for those who are targeted. Understand that there are no innocent bystanders when it comes to bullying. We can have compassion for kids who turn to bullying behavior out of their own internal pain, but parents and kids alike must take a stand and say "No more bullying!" Not my kid, and not your kid, either.

36

PEACE OF MIND:
A SANCTUARY INSIDE

Having peace of mind doesn't just happen when everything in life falls magically in order. (When does that ever happen anyhow?) As mothers, we cannot wait for the events in our lives to stop, or for adverse circumstances to change before we look for peace of mind. We must instead create space within that allows us to be in the center of the whirlpool of ten thousand activities and tasks without getting lost, and this takes practice.

Peace of mind happens from finding stillness within and calming your monkey mind, avoiding worry and not allowing outside chaos to penetrate your inner sanctuary. Cultivating this peaceful place inside is an activity that takes about ten minutes of practice a day. If you can do ten minutes when you wake up, and ten when you go to sleep, all the better. Here's what I suggest:

Create a ritual with the intention of cultivating an inner sanctuary. Wake up and make yourself something hot and soothing to drink. Go back to bed, or to a quiet room or corner or a personal space you have that is just yours, and sit comfortably as you enjoy slowly sipping your drink. Notice your state of mind. Are you rested and calm, or are you worried and ragged? Are you angry or sad or tense? Whatever you are feeling, just take the time to sit with it and breathe and be present with your feelings.

In another chapter, we discuss how to deep-belly breathe. Close your eyes, take ten of those deep breaths in, breathing sunlight in and out, making the exhale long and expansive so as to release any anxiety and tension. Feel supported by a tree of light behind you, and see the tree branching out around you. Continue to breathe in sunlight and exhale deeply until you feel grounded and relaxed. Ask the tree to support any worries and concerns you have and to take the tension from your body. Ask to be shown your inner sanctuary, and keep a journal nearby to write down what your special place looks and feels like. Is it near a river or the ocean? Does it sit in a valley or on a mountaintop, or in a garden? After you spend some time there, breathing in sunlight and enjoying the respite of this place, thank your tree for supporting you, and thank this sanctuary for revealing itself. Make a note of how you are feeling now, and resolve to return to this feeling of safe calm through your breath throughout your day. Breathe, and find peace of mind inside. Return to this ritual again at the end of the day, before you sleep.

When you practice this simple meditation as a ritual, this peaceful place is where you can return throughout your day. Isn't it lovely that you don't have to go anywhere to get it? It's simple and it's your sanctuary of peace inside.

37

SEEING OUR KIDS AS
UNIQUE INDIVIDUALS

I've often thought how nice it would be if each of our children came with their own instruction booklet on how to raise them. Drawing from both parents' lineage, you just never know what you're going to get, and each child is surely a unique individual.

Ideally, we should help our children find their gifts and share them with the world, and this is in fact the goal, isn't it? I can never understand it when someone makes the statement "I parented my children exactly the same way," and then wonders how they turned out so different. Parenting is actually as much an investigation into our children's internal workings as it is a job caring for their nutrition, education, health, and housing. As moms, we need to see each child as he or she is, not as we imagine or hope they are; and a large part of that is seeing them as completely separate individuals from their siblings and not as extensions of ourselves. Each one of us is uniquely and differently designed. And this truth adds an entirely new dimension to our job as Mom.

I've witnessed what happens in families where the parents lay down the law and govern the household with fixed rules and principles that don't provide an environment that is at all adaptive to the child. Remember that old adage about trying to fit a round peg into a square hole? Well, in one family I know, I saw one out of three children adapt well to this highly structured box. The other two did not. Arguments and rebellions followed. Now, as adults, they are struggling to find their way.

A certain amount of conformity is necessary to life. We call this socialization, and civilizations depend on it. But we also want to encourage the individuality that comes through differentiation. That is what produces the great masterpieces of art, architecture, music, and literature. It is the thinking and dreaming that took us to the moon, and into cyberspace. Our children are like snowflakes and fingerprints; no two are alike. And that is a good thing. As a mother, it always seemed to me that my job was to create an environment where each of my two much-loved but strikingly different daughters could thrive. The concept of home was adaptive. Each had to feel that this was that soft place where they could be who they were, no questions asked, no judgment—just love.

Here's a simple example of what I mean about shifting the environmental structure to meet your child's needs. One of your children may need to burn off a lot of energy, and therefore thrives on a schedule loaded with high activity. Another child may need more downtime to play in his room, to explore his world through books, or with his hands through projects or with LEGOs. One child I know designed entire LEGO cities that took up the floor space of his family's finished basement. There were many times his mother would have loved to move "the city," but she never did. Today, that child is a successful urban planner. The takeaway is this: Your kids will always let you know what they need by their level of happiness and cooperation. They may not do this with words, but their temperaments and behavior will tell you loud and clear, I need activity! Or, Please don't overschedule my day.

Identifying what kind of learner your child is can really help you create the right environment for them. There are many ways we learn: visually, auditorily, or kinesthetically (through movement), to name a few. Chances are, we are dominant learners in one of these areas. In the last decade, education specialists have suggested that the surge in children diagnosed with learning disabilities may really be as much a function of curriculum and teaching that fail to account for differences in children's learning styles as anything inherently "wrong" with the child. Who your child is, and what feeds him or her best, are important questions you must answer. As you find the path that best serves his or her distinct personality, you will be writing your own instruction manual for raising your child—one that no other manual could, or should, ever duplicate.

38

WHEN KIDS MAKE MISTAKES

It's often difficult for us to separate our own identity from that of our child. We are so invested in their lives that we become attached to their behavior and how it may reflect on us, as if we were being graded for their achievements or failures. But kids make mistakes; their formative years will be full of dramas. They may behave badly and hurt the feelings of other children; they may behave unethically and cheat on a test or plagiarize a school report; they may behave in socially inappropriate ways, posting questionable material on a social network site. They may cut class or get drunk or get into a fender bender. When these things happen, we have to take a step back and remind ourselves that they have a life and a journey that is separate from our own. We need to not only be invested in their successes, but also remember that learning from their mistakes is also its own kind of success.

A good friend shared an important learning experience with me— one that was painful for her because in hindsight she would have handled herself differently. (Haven't we all been there?) Her daughter came home from school one day in tears. She had been playing with her flip camera earlier that week, and had sent an inappropriate picture of herself to a boy she liked. The boy then turned around and posted it on the Internet. Most of the seventh-grade class saw it. Humiliated and hysterical when she learned about this at school, she went to talk to the school counselor, who was very firm with her but also compassionate and kind. My friend, however, did not have the same reaction. Shocked and angry that her daughter could do something like that, she berated her child—loudly— that afternoon, telling her what a stupid thing that was to do and how hard it was to come back from a bad reputation. The daughter burst into tears and ran out of the room. "Thanks a lot. You can't quit, can you? My counselor was much nicer than you are!" And my friend responded by shouting back, "She wouldn't have been if it was her daughter!"

Now, my friend had every reason to be upset and disappointed with her child. But as she reflected back on the incident that evening, after her temper had cooled, my friend realized that her daughter was already suffering the consequences of her own actions. She already knew she had made a mistake and was feeling remorseful. The teaching had already been done, and so it hadn't helped the situation for her mother to berate her further. Instead of a lesson being learned, the daughter's self-esteem further worsened. The girl saw herself as a bad person, when in fact she'd just made a mistake. In this incident, my friend learned something, too—to show compassion when a child is already hurting, and to know when to step back and say, "She's already received the lesson." The discipline is already done when the natural consequences of embarrassment and humiliation hit the mark straight through the heart.

If my friend had had a redo, rather than go into "How could you?" mode, she would have offered comfort and supportive reassurance, holding space for her daughter's adolescent growing pains. As parents, we can't help but want to protect our children from mistakes and failure that can be damaging socially and otherwise, but we are also the only ones who can create the space for their healing. When we are attached, we take our children's actions personally, and what we are really saying in that moment when we lack compassion is "This behavior is a bad reflection on me." If we can step back and remember our own mistakes, we can offer a good dose of compassionate understanding instead of taking our kids' mistakes personally and reacting from the fear of failure that we see in their reflection.

39

KEEP THE LINES OF
COMMUNICATION OPEN

There are few things more important in doing the best job we can with our kids than keeping the lines of communication open. I have had hundreds of positive and surely just as many negative conversations with my daughters over the years, and perhaps what I value most about our relationship is knowing that they know they can talk to me. When communication breaks down between you and your child, it's up to you as the parent to make the shifts and adjustments necessary to get back on track and reopen the conversation. You want to keep those lines of communication always open so you can respond and interact with love.

Something happens when our kids reach a certain age. All of a sudden they seem to look at us like we are aliens from a different planet. We go from being the authority on everything (remember those infinite number of "Why, Mommy" questions they had as three-year-olds?) to their thinking that we don't know anything at all. While we can be puzzled and hurt by the warp-like speed in which our opinions and knowledge are diminished in their eyes, no alarm bells need to go off. It is normal for tweens and teens to look to their friends first for connection and advice, but we need to remain a clear and strong influence in their lives and to make sure they keep talking to us.

Your relationship with your child is a two-way street. Good communication is about dialogue, not lectures. It's never too late to establish new habits, and the seeds of great communication can be planted when your kids are very young. They can also grow and change as you implement consistent new ways to speak and listen. It's amazing what can happen to your communication when you make a minor shift in yourself; it changes how you and your child relate to one another.

The best moms I know start speaking with their children when they are young. They ask questions and then pause and listen—really listen—to the responses. Children intuitively know when adults respect and understand them; relationships do, after all, have to do with relating to one another. Here are a few things I have seen that parents do to increase their "relatability" factor and their odds that they will likely have effective communication with their kids at any age:

1. They are not rigid rule-makers without backing up their rules with good reason and thoughtful communication.
2. They use reasonable consequences when disciplining. The crime must match the punishment.
3. They don't yell reactively and fly off the handle on a regular basis. (Even though everyone loses it now and then!)

4. They are really good listeners even amidst a conflict; they listen without judgment.
5. They don't talk to their children as if they are stupid.
6. They create a safe environment in which to have a difficult conversation. This includes attentive listening on your part. By "active listening," you reflect back to your child what you have just heard, in words he would agree with. When we do this, we are assuring our child we have listened to him attentively. We are showing him we understand what he has said, as opposed to what we thought he might have said.
7. They don't live by the philosophy: "You won't win, because I'm the parent and I'm always right." While the home may not be a democracy, it's not a dictatorship, either.
8. Parents respect appropriate boundaries. Children are entitled to their privacy as long as they have not shown you any reason not to be. Moms build a deep level of trust by asking before invading.
9. When their kids need to be disciplined, they explain why the behavior isn't appropriate. And they give their kids the opportunity for rebuttal, even if the consequences will be the same.
10. They enlist their children in solving problems, creating boundaries, and establishing consequences for breaking those guidelines.
11. They ask about "feelings." By asking a lot of questions and making it safe to express feelings, a safety net is created that helps the children to speak out and trust more. The barrier between adult

and child is shortened because the child knows his or her feelings are acknowledged.

12. In a conflict: They allow it to be safe for their kids to express their feelings before they expect them to be rational and conversational. Often, if there is a bit of space between you and your child after a conflict, the dust settles, and it's easier to enroll them in a two-way conversation where you both are listening and speaking.

If you want to keep your lines of communication open, it's important to recognize that lecturing your kids won't work for them—not at any age. If you get on a bandwagon and fail to allow communication to flow respectfully and naturally, you may squelch your child's voice or teach her to act out in rebellion. In your manner of communication you must be firm, loving, guiding, responsive, approachable, and, when it's deserved, you must be able to laugh at yourself and apologize easily. You want to be committed to consistency and to becoming a truly good listener, most of the time. Kids are just like all people; we all want to be heard. Finally, always try to listen and respond with love. Most interactions that start with love end with love, so keep your children talking to you by being open to hearing what they have to say.

40

RECLAIM YOUR FAMILY TIME

✿ While doing a book interview last year for *Don't Sweat the Small Stuff for Women,* I met Dana Hilmer, an author and Internet radio host of the LifestyleMom Radio Café, who is launching a movement called "Take Back Family Time."

Now, there's an idea we can all relate to. I can speak from experience when I say that if you could fast-forward your life, you would never look back and regret the time you spent sitting around the kitchen table with your family, taking family vacations, or just hanging out together on a lazy afternoon. You will never meet a person who, at the end of life, says, "I wish I had spent less time with my kids, and more time at work." Yet, every day in a busy house feels like a speed race that takes every person in a different direction.

Here are some ideas on how to reclaim your family time:

1. Make family dinners a priority. Eat together at least three times a week, including Sundays.

2. Plan a family fun activity every weekend that lasts at least a couple of hours. Quality time together might include playing a board game; enjoying a movie night; reading a book out loud together (such as one of the Harry Potter series); or an outdoor activity like gardening, hiking, biking, or skiing.

3. Declare Sundays "a tech-free day"—no cell phones, computers, iPods, or TVs. (That means you, too: Put away that BlackBerry!)

4. Encourage kids to support their siblings in their extracurricular activities by being present as a spectator at games, presentations, and recitals.

5. Have your house be the place for the friends to hang out.

6. Prepare a wall calendar and fill in the monthly schedule of each family member with color-coded marker. See where and what can be cut back so you can all spend more time together.

7. Try to keep summers relatively unstructured. Celebrate spontaneity and improvisation.

8. Create your own rituals and traditions as a family, regarding holidays, vacations, and special occasions. These are repeated ceremonies and gestures that create strong bonds and memories which, in turn, can be passed down to your children's children.

9. Always celebrate birthdays together as a family—no matter what is involved to clear the plate for the evening.

10. Share a long-term family project—involve the entire family in making scrapbooks to preserve the memory of a special person or to record a vacation or an occasion. Plan a garden or a social

action project. Spend a day together working at a Habitat for Humanity site. Conduct a day of interviews with older relatives and create an oral history of your family.

Looking back, I relish the times we had as a family playing Monopoly (even though Kenna always got mad that someone else had more properties than she had). I cherish the sandcastles we made on the beach and the long walks we took with the girls in their little red wagon. I will always remember riding horses together, carving pumpkins, coloring Easter eggs, decorating gingerbread houses, and playing hide-and-seek in the trees. Once upon a time, we had so much fun as a family. Don't let the business of life or school or career steal these times from you. Life is too short, and it all passes quickly by. You will never regret taking back your family time and creating those moments in life that make childhood a cherished memory for you and your kids.

41

CELEBRATE OTHER MOTHERS

❀ When I gave birth to Jasmine and Kenna, I said to Richard: "It should be front page news every time a woman does that!" Over the years that followed, I realized that giving birth is the easy part!

Being a mother is a round-the-clock job. There are no sick days, no vacations, no personal days. Whether you have a partner or not, this job requires tenacity, patience, creative problem-solving, great listening and communication skills, tremendous physical stamina, and emotional resolve, not to mention running the household and staying on top of the laundry. The rewards are intrinsic; but a job well done is not always recognized or quantifiable. Nonetheless, it's the most important job there is. That's why it's so essential for us to celebrate our sisters and to acknowledge other moms for what they do by giving them a compliment.

I'm not talking about Hallmark moments and the kind of cards-and-flowers recognition moms receive on Mother's Day from their families. Instead, I'm thinking about what we as women can do for each other to show our encouragement during the rest of the year. That is because, though we may not have a lot in common and may live our lives under very different circumstances, every encounter with a mother is an opportunity to celebrate our common journey and reinforce what an incredible impact we have on the world as we serve our families with love and kindness.

One of the greatest gifts you can give another woman is to notice and tell her what a great mother she is. My own daughter, who is now a mom herself, often sends me text messages telling me what a great mother I am and have always been. That never fails to put a smile on my face and warm my heart. And when I am with her and see the beautiful way she is raising my grandson, I remember to do the same for her. There's nothing more affirmative than receiving a pat on the back from another mother—especially from your own.

I notice the exceptional care that many of my friends give to their kids and the strategies they use every day to make and manage the best home and family life they can. I always make it a point to celebrate them with a compliment: "Wow, I don't know if you realize it or not, but you are such a great mom. You remain so cheerful at the five o'clock hour, and I love the patience you show with your kids even when you are cooking dinner and overseeing homework." I also share my admiration for the many interesting and original ways they enrich their children's lives. One friend takes extra-special care and makes fruit kabobs with fresh melon, strawberries, and pineapple on skewers for a healthy birthday snack at school parties; another creates handmade family albums of important holidays, family trips, and summer vacations. Each child is assigned a "day," and writes a short description of that day's activities. At the end of the week, the entire family votes on the best day, meal, activity, and the funniest moment—all recorded on the last page of the album. My friend's clever idea preserves memories while also giving each child a chance to be in charge, and to learn responsibility. It's all about observing, sharing, and remembering to recognize the good things moms do.

When you celebrate other mothers, you will be surprised about the benefits it brings to your own parenting, and to your feelings about the job you're doing as a mom. When we compliment someone else, the simple act of noticing what they do right affects how we do things ourselves. As I notice the positive things my friends are doing with their kids, I can't help but mimic those qualities in my own parenting. We see in others empathetic reflections of ourselves. It's impossible to see in someone else a quality that is not present in yourself. By observing and complimenting one another, we see what great mothers we are and realize what even better moms we can be!

42

THE POWER OF PRAYER
IS IN THE ASKING

I spent most of my early life being really good at using prayer to ask for assistance. Then, I became a mom and somehow, I inadvertently adopted the philosophy: When all else fails, then pray. I'm not really clear why I changed a system that seemed to work really well at helping me overcome my self-doubt. I guess I didn't feel there was room for insecurity in parenting, and that I had to have all the answers in order to be a good mother. But perhaps what I needed most, sometimes, was the humility to realize that the opposite was true. You don't have to have all the answers; you have to be open to receiving them.

Looking back now, I realize that a lot of the fun of motherhood can be diminished by the resentment you feel in being always responsible. If you feel the weight of your duties and wear them like an extra skin, you can feel overworked and exhausted much of the time. I have come to understand that mothering takes a lot of faith in something.

When I am deeply troubled, I like to think of myself by the sea with a fishing rod in my hand. I cast the line almost as an act of surrender. Each thought goes with it, releasing all of my concerns, worries, and responsibilities. I just let it all go and allow faith to bring me back to myself again. As I cast out my prayer, it is a request for assistance. As mothers, we find it inexplicably difficult to ask for anything. But the power of prayer, I have found, takes all the weight off your shoulders and releases you from the burden of having to know everything all the time. When I pray and let go, I am shedding that extra layer of worry, and I just feel better.

I like to think of myself as a well-seasoned woman—a grandmother, a widow, and a single mother to my children. Each morning when I rise, my personal prayer is: "Divine love, play me as an instrument in your finely tuned orchestra of life. Show me how to serve love today. Thy will, not my will, be done this day." I surrender and trust that there is a beneficent plan for me and my children, something better, more profound and complete than anything I could devise. All I have to do is show up and be myself.

Prayer is also cleansing. As moms, our days are as packed as our heads; there is so little downtime, and our worries and concerns can divert us from our inner wisdom. Prayer can clear the mind of clutter and allow each of us to be an empty container, able to hold compassion and the unconditional love that our families need. It's helpful to remind ourselves that there is perfection in the imperfect journey of life, and that prayer is the leap of faith that helps us let go of the illusion of control.

When we do, we open to being able to feel the liberty that comes from release and the warmth of the energy that moves gently yet inexorably inside our being. When we confront life with vulnerability and ask for assistance, this allows us to be guided to the answers to our questions, and ultimately helps us to let go of the worry that can steal our joy.

43

HOW TO SPEAK TO OUR KIDS
ABOUT THE BIG STUFF

✿ There's no easy way to speak with children about loss of any kind, and there are different types of heartbreak. One of the ways you can prepare to speak to your children about the big stuff is to help them understand that all things in life are temporary, and that while change and transition can be painful, these are natural to life, too. As you define your spiritual values, you will be better able to speak to your children about loss, grief, and matters of the heart.

Nature shows us how everything changes form. As raindrops fall in winter, they turn to ice and snow, and the snow in turn melts in the spring and returns to water again. These cycles of life are inevitable in nature and to all forms of life. One of our cultural misnomers is to deny the idea of our mortality in an attempt to shield ourselves and our children from a part of life that we naturally cycle through, just like nature.

We do not serve our children by living in denial of death. Researchers have found that there is a higher incidence of happy people in cultures that teach children to be fully aware that they or someone they love could die any day. It isn't morbid to speak of death and its possibility to our kids; it is a reality, and of course it will always hold the pain of grief. But isolating our children from death neither protects nor prepares them for life's painful realities, and there are many other kinds of losses that happen along the way.

After my husband's death, telling my children that their father had died was probably the most difficult moment of my life. I remember knowing that there was no saving them from the pain of loss now, but I allowed my intuition to guide me and began speaking of love. I said: "No matter what happens, you know one thing, and that is how much your daddy loves you and you love him. Love never dies." In the beginning, I focused on creating a safe container, a secure environment for my daughters in which they could grieve. I noticed that teenagers could only hold so much of this process and that, as time marched on, life would sporadically trigger their grief in small doses.

I felt that the best way for them to let out their grief was to encourage them to express their feelings, and I, their mother who was also in grief, would hold their space without trying to fix things. This made it safe to feel pain so that they, too, could heal. The pain of loss is not something that can be airbrushed away; it is felt in real time. Grief is an individual process which each of us must find our own expression of and way through. There is no one way to speak about loss, and there is no rescuing anyone from grief.

Grief comes as a friend to help us endure the changes we haven't yet accepted. Sometimes the most we can do is make it safe for grief to come. It has its own agenda and will show up in its own time. The best thing to do is to welcome the wave, surrender to it, and allow it to liberate you from the clutches of loss. While letting go is very difficult for adults, it is even more so for older children, especially teens, as they usually have not yet developed a spiritual practice and philosophy, and their emotional fitness to handle loss is still evolving. They are, after all, still children. This being true, I have always encouraged my kids to write in journals and speak to their father as if he is present.

Children of all ages relate to the idea of the presence of angels, and feelings of love which, while one can't see them, are nonetheless present. This can be a comforting way to speak to kids about the continued presence of their loved ones. We can teach them about the deeper connections we can access within, and they can learn to trust in what they cannot see but in what they can feel. It is most important to always make it safe for them to experience their feelings and find healthy means of expression. Express it out, or depress it in.

It takes some time and practice to define and cultivate your spiritual beliefs. As you do this, it will help you to guide your children when the inevitable big stuff happens and you must find the best words to begin a very deep process. Like adults, children find their own way through these difficult transitions in their own time. My personal comfort is that love is eternal; this is the greatest teaching in any loss. While all things change form, love is formless. All of the things we have enjoyed in life, we carry in our hearts forever.

· 44 ·

TODAY'S WOMAN, TODAY'S MOM

The identification with being a mom is a powerful one. Our role is clear: We are caretakers, nurses, counselors, and teachers. We are chefs, home organizers, personal assistants, and coaches. We wear so many hats as a mom that it's easy to forget we once had a life on our own, before kids. Motherhood is so occupying that it's challenging to bring it into balance with our other aspects—our sensuality as women, our need to find expression for our intellect and creativity, our careers, and our desire to serve our greater community. Yet these are the yin and yang qualities that paint the portrait of a complete woman—a woman and a mom today.

Contrary to what happens sometimes, being a mom does not mean that sensuality has to get thrown under the bus. Okay, leaking breasts and a newborn clamoring for her next meal won't exactly nourish that side of you, and the busyness of our complicated lives can leave us just too tired to care about our appearance or our sexual needs. But just as a rose needs water to stay lush, our feminine side needs nourishment to maintain its luster, too. While self-care may seem impossibly time-consuming, there are simple things you can do to just feel good about yourself as a woman each day, cultivating those sensual feelings through small acts. When your hair is cut and your nails are trim, you may feel more womanly. Try lighting candles in the evening after the kids are in bed, taking a long soaking bath, and wearing good lingerie (something that feels beautiful to you), or a soft flowing blouse during the day. The feel of silk, lace, or fine cotton against your skin will remind you that there is a feminine dimension to your life that hasn't gone totally underground. Treat yourself as you treat others in your life—with gentle kindness.

A woman's joy is also nourished by the life she makes outside her family. Though time is precious, many women are inspired to give back to their communities through some form of philanthropic work. One friend has used her legal skills to help create a foundation for her school district; another friend is on the board of her local library; another has helped create a summer program for children of low-income families. Other women participate in book clubs that allow them to read widely on a range of interesting topics and to discuss them—something they value not only because they are giving expression to their intellectual sides, but also because it connects them with other like-minded women. While some of us have more time than others, may just be better organized, able to compartmentalize, or just feel the call more urgently, when we give ourselves permission and step outside our lives as moms—while the kids are at school, or with the help of babysitters or our partners, or after dinner for the occasional committee or board meeting—we do two things: We maintain an identity outside of our home and work lives, and we set an example for our kids. We are sending them a message that living a full life isn't only about raising our children, and that when they become adults, there will be expectations about helping others in our extended community, too.

My remarkable friend Laura makes time in her busy life to volunteer at a soup kitchen and organizes in-kind donations from local restaurants; she also serves on various school committees, and is a board member of a crisis intervention center. She added out-of-home activities gradually because, honestly, when we are in the thick of raising very young children, there isn't a lot of idle time. But she shared with me the Mother's Day card she received this year from her son. It read: "I'm so proud of you, Mom, for all you do for our family but also, what you do for everyone else." One might also say that she feels what she does is as much for herself as it is for others. As she is making a difference in their lives, she is also expanding her own.

We are complex individuals with many needs and many aspects to our being. There is one thing I know for certain: While your children love your attention, they don't want all the focus of your attention on them all the time. It places too much pressure on them to please, and inhibits them from becoming independent from you, if you hover too close. That said, if someone were to ask you to strip off all of those hats you wear as a mom to show them the ones you wear outside of motherhood, what would those hats look like and how many would there be? How can you give more complete expression to the fullness of the woman you are? What nourishes your spirit outside of being a mother? And, as we strive to balance all the components of ourselves as women, are you replenishing your sensuality in small ways? How are you taking care of your body, your spirit, and your mind? As you take inventory of the answers to these questions and fill in the gaps, they will integrate into one, and bring you to the balance in being a woman and also being a mom.

45

STEP OFF YOUR MERRY-GO-ROUND

❀ Understanding the nature of thought is an important aspect of keeping life in perspective. It's so easy to get caught up in cyclical thinking without even realizing it. A "thought attack" is cyclical thinking that feels like you are spinning on a merry-go-round that doesn't take you anywhere but in a circle. In order to access your wisdom and common sense, you need to step off the merry-go-round and break the chain of circular thinking, to relieve yourself of the stress, anxiety, and worry that comes from getting caught up in fear.

As new mothers, we've all been plagued by "what if" thinking. We bring our babies home and are consumed with worry, very likely because, deep down, we don't feel confident in our ability to take care of a newborn. They look so delicate and helpless; but indeed their lungs are the first indicator that they are not so fragile. In fact, babies are geared for survival—something we new moms learn that first week.

And as moms, we all fall victim to "what if this should happen" thinking because of generations of genetic coding that enables us to sense the things that may be harmful to our children. As a result of this, many of us see our job as keeping ten steps ahead of our little ones to protect them from harm due to injury or illness. Protecting our children is a natural instinct and a necessary role, but when we climb onto a merry-go-round of worry, we lose perspective and joy. Yes, the road through childhood is bumpy and filled with obstacles, but deep down, we know most of the things we worry about may never happen, and if they do, we have a much higher chance of solving them efficiently when we are not caught in a "thought attack" provoked by anxiety.

Melissa was a new mom. She was anxious from the moment she found out she was pregnant. She took wonderful care of herself and gave birth to a healthy boy. Chad's infancy coincided, however, with the peak flu season, and there was a lot of media attention about a "new" flu that was spreading in epidemic proportions. A young mother, Melissa was understandably concerned and would be cautious, but she became over-whelmed by anxiety attacks that her baby would get the flu, to the extent that she couldn't sleep. She went to extreme and unbalanced measures and allowed no one into her home, and she never took the baby out for fresh air, either. Her "what if" thought attacks were not doing anything to keep her baby safe, but they were driving her and her husband crazy. Finally, Melissa was able to see what these all-consuming patterns of thought and fear were doing to her and how they were interfering with the beauty of her experience of having a newborn.

One might argue that she's a better mother because she worries about things, but that's not true, because often your fear clouds your innate wisdom and your judgment. You can and should always take common-sense, instinctual steps to keep your children safe. When you do this without fear, your ability to be present and joyful while you are taking care of your child is enhanced. As we talked about earlier, the empowered mom is responsive, not reactive.

Self-talk can help you walk the walk. You can step down and out of your thought attack simply through awareness. I often say to myself when I'm on my merry-go-round, "Aw, there you go again, Kris. I know exactly where this line of thinking is taking you." Remember that the worry and anxiety aren't going to reveal the solution to your problems as much as they will drive you crazy. As you see the thoughts of worry go around and around, you can stop the merry-go-round and step off at any point. As you notice your "what if" chain of worry, each thought connecting to another like horses in a line, remember that you have hold of the reins. Pull the reins in and get yourself off the merry-go-round, returning to the magic of the here and now where life is good.

46

WHEN TEENS WANT TO PARTY

❀ Just as our kids seem to grow right before our eyes, their parties also change as they get older. When our kids become teens, the fun superhero or princess costumes are replaced with provocative ones, while the juice and soda are possibly spiked with alcohol. As parents, we find ourselves in a position to give our kids the opportunity for fun and celebration, while protecting them from harm, and ourselves from liability.

I had heard the stories when my girls were in high school about the "cool" moms who allowed their kids to drink as long as the kids stayed under the parents' watchful eyes. I felt quite differently, and I certainly didn't want to be seen as a "cool" mom by the high school crowd. As a single mom on my own, I felt sure that I would be outnumbered and without help if things got out of hand, so I prohibited large groups of kids from congregating at my house. When Kenna was turning eighteen, she really wanted to celebrate with a theme party. The thought of this terrified me, as I had recently become aware of the new liability laws for parents who in any way facilitated underage drinking in their homes. This was just the situation I had sought to avoid because I knew kids would drink alcohol overtly or covertly, whether or not I was there to chaperone. And yet, I didn't want to disappoint Kenna, and I wanted to celebrate her.

So, I rounded up a posse of other moms to help me chaperone, and laid down some ground rules. Kenna had to agree that the invitations would specifically say that there would be no alcohol allowed, and that every kid attending needed to have a designated driver. I was very clear: If Kenna didn't like my rules, then no party. It's also important for teens to understand the risks to you as the parent if something goes terribly wrong, including the possibility of jail time and losing everything you have worked hard for. I was most concerned with kids who drink and drive, and their safety. Even though I wasn't serving alcohol, I knew they would probably smuggle their contraband in, so I prepared myself. Here is a list of the things I did to maximize the fun and minimize the danger:

- The theme was animal print, and everyone dressed in costume.
- I moved my furniture out of the house and made the living room a dance floor.
- I rented a couple of fun disco lights and set up heat lamps outside on the patio.
- I locked the bedrooms, so that kids stayed in open areas where they could be seen.

- I had plenty of food that the kids like, and did a Costco run. I served snack food that lasted all night long: pizza, veggies, sodas, brownies, candy, and chips.
- Every guest was assigned a designated driver. There was a list of drivers and their passengers. I had someone standing at the door as the kids came in. Car keys had to be checked and left with a chaperone assigned to the door, and each guest had to sign in before they could be admitted.
- In order to retrieve their keys, every driver on the list knew in advance they would have to blow into a Breathalyzer at the end of night. They had to test at a 0.0, or we would find them and their assigned passengers a ride home. The driver would have to pick up the car in the morning. (By the way, you can pick up an inexpensive Breathalyzer online, or through companies like The Sharper Image.)
- I covered any upholstered furniture remaining in the party area to protect it from spills.
- I locked up my valuables (jewelry, etc.).
- We checked bags and purses, and took water bottles and open bottles at the door, because the kids often fill them with vodka and other clear liquors.
- My posse of moms was visible all night long, circulating the great room and checking the closed doors. They weren't shy about confiscating any bottle that looked suspicious, or opening the bathroom door if there was a group of kids in there too long.
- We ended the party at midnight.

As our children grow, the boundaries we set for them change, too. They change as children earn more responsibility. But we must never forget that while other people's children are not our own, in the eyes of the law, they are ours as long as they are under our roofs. Moreover, we have a moral responsibility to other children's parents to protect them, as we would want them to protect our children. We all must share the same concern, and that is to keep our young people safe . . . even if doing so makes us not "cool." A partying teen will be a partying teen, but with planning and diligence, you can help them have a great time. Be smart. Keep it fun, keep it dry, and keep it legal.

47

LIFELINE SUNDAYS

✿ When I was a young woman, I was a bit of a workaholic and I burned the candle at both ends. It seemed that I had to catch a cold or virus before I would take some time off to rest. However, this unconscious system of driving myself to exhaustion wasn't workable for the adult version of me. As a mom, I have had to learn that preemptive rest before waiting to collapse is key to a family's overall health and equanimity. In time, I learned that I needed one day of rest, and these became my "lifeline" Sundays.

This insight came to me when Richard was out of town and my girls were six and three-and-a-half years old. I remember thinking: *I am so exhausted.* What I needed most was to stay in bed and rest and read. I woke up instead with a 104° fever and a sore throat, and I couldn't get out of bed. Illness is no fun, but being sick and a mom without help is the worst. I did my best to drag my aching body out of bed long enough to take care of the kids' basic needs, but when Richard returned home two days later, there was pancake batter all over the kitchen and bowls of half-eaten cereal with milk on the kitchen counter; the television was blaring, and the kids looked disheveled. Being sick wasn't rest any longer.

In my youth, well before kids, I might have been able to run myself ragged, but now I could clearly see that this way of being no longer served me or my family. I decided that instead of waiting for exhaustion or illness to take a break, I would have "lifeline" Sundays where I gave myself permission to have a pajama day, for at least half the day. This meant I could close my door and be alone and sleep or just have quiet time to nap, meditate, read, and listen to music or watch Lifetime movies. When I was a schoolgirl, my favorite thing to do when I wasn't feeling well was to stay home and, tucked into bed or on the couch with my pillow and blanket, spend the day watching "the oldies but the goodies" movies, one right after the other. Realizing the need for downtime was an *Aha!* moment for me. (Note to self: You don't have to get ill to rest.)

My family learned that Sundays were a lifeline day for me. Richard was in charge. They either joined my pajama party, or they did their own thing, but Sunday became our day to rejuvenate from the grind of our busy routines. This rest provided for some great family cuddle time, and some much needed relaxation that helped us restore harmony to the hectic pace we kept up all week.

48

WHEN ALL ELSE FAILS, LAUGH

✿ It's often not the mountain that gets you. It's the pebble in your shoe. We can generally rally for the big stuff of life, but this is a book about how not to let the little things get to you. When I talk to my friends, they all agree that it's the small events that can throw us off balance and make us lose focus on the big picture. On those days when everything seems to be going wrong—or does go wrong—you just have to step back and laugh. Laughter is a great healer. It lets out pressure and stress, and restores perspective. It's as essential to your well-being as vitamin C.

My girlfriend Lucy is the mom of four busy kids. She begins her routine every day aware that something unforeseen will come up to disrupt the flow of her day. One child is ill, and another forgets his homework. The dog throws up and needs to go to the vet. Somebody spills their smoothie all over herself and her sister's backpack while you are driving them home from soccer practice. The car-pool mother is sick. Your oldest daughter needs to be picked up from the math tutor, and your little one needs to be dropped off at ballet. Every day introduces new chaos amidst the order in her home (trust me, this woman is one of the most organized people alive), yet she can do little but laugh and stay flexible in the moment.

Then there is Robin, a media executive, who walked into her office one morning to a ringing telephone. It was the babysitter. "Do you have Carly's homework?" she asked. "What are you talking about?" Robin responded as she began rummaging through her briefcase. Sure enough, she did! And eight-year-old Carly had the page of handwritten notes that Robin had made for this morning's presentation while the two sat together the night before at the kitchen table, each of them doing their work. Somehow, as she'd raced out of the house this morning, she'd scooped up the wrong papers. Robin might have cried, but instead she laughed. As she told me later, "Stuff happens. No one was sick. No one died. And, fortunately, I still have my job."

If you desire peace and happiness, it's all about keeping the small stuff small. Happiness is not a pursuit where things in life go your way, it's about keeping your perspective. On any given day, you've got to take a deep breath and remember to laugh, because if you don't, the mishaps can mushroom into disasters and leave you frustrated and angry. Those pent up emotions will spiral, carrying you further down into a lower mood. Often, when we are low, all we see is what's wrong, because that's where our vision is. Conversely, when we laugh, we lighten our moods. Being able to shake off the small stuff increases your resiliency and stamina. As Charles Darwin said: "It is not the strongest of the species that survives, nor the most intelligent that survives, it is the one that is the most adaptable to change."

Don't worry if you lose perspective, because every day is a new day. Small stuff will happen—it's the law of nature. Find the humor in most situations and laugh out loud, and you will maintain your equilibrium as you steer your course through those seemingly out-of-control, rougher days.

49

IF YOU WANT TO BE ON FACEBOOK, I'M GOING TO BE YOUR FRIEND

I joined Facebook for business reasons, and when my friends heard about it, they said, "Welcome to your new obsession." It didn't take me long to understand why Facebook is so popular with Gen X-ers. Connection and friendship are so important to all of us, but to our youth, popularity is everything.

It's challenging to attempt to address social media in a protective way that we can feel good about. Once your kids become tweens, it is all but impossible to prohibit them from the Internet, and they become very savvy about how to get around restrictions. Yet it can be a mecca for pedophiles, stalkers, and Internet creepers. It's up to you to exercise vigilance and know how to put parental restrictions in place.

We've all heard the terrible stories about cyber-bullying. My own family was touched by it; both our girls dealt with being publicly ostracized, threatened, and bullied online. One day, several years ago, Jazz was being harassed on Myspace. At the time, we barely knew what Myspace was, but we did know that our daughter was enthralled with it. It wasn't until she was threatened and ganged up on, however, that we realized how harmful social networking sites could be.

I recently asked my girlfriend, the mother of two daughters and a son who are all in their teens, how she manages to patrol their use of social media. She tells them, "You wanna be on Facebook? No problem, but I'm going to be your friend."

What that means is that she regularly peruses her kids' Facebook pages to make sure they are being appropriate and that their friends are, too. My friend confided that she began to do so after she'd noticed that her son was suddenly acting strangely—withdrawn and sad. That wasn't like him, but he wouldn't tell her what was wrong. Then she went on Facebook and realized that some boys were making some mean comments about him, trying to take him down a social notch. Ironically, my friend felt grateful to Facebook, since it makes it possible for parents to see what kids are thinking and feeling that they may not otherwise be so free to express. It's important, though, for parents to keep a low profile about checking up on them, so that their children don't clam up too hard and communication between you remains open.

We had enough evidence from social media threats to get a restraining order against the girl who was bullying and harassing Jazz at school. Cyber-bullying has been very damaging to many kids, and that's why it's so important to be aware of what is taking place in cyberspace.

While we can't control every conversation our children have, we can keep pace with their changing profiles. My daughters have grown up with the new technology and are conversant in it. We parents will have to grow with them and become conversant, too, or be left behind, no matter the facts. They will have more "friends" than I could ever imagine, and their personal lives and social profiles are put out there as naturally as we listed ourselves in the telephone pages.

There is an art to allowing your kids to engage with the social media without controlling every move they make. There is a fine line between trust, and the privacy we believe people are entitled to, and our instinct—and job—to keep our children safe. It's important for them to know this, and you should make it a point to have a conversation about the appropriate use of social media. Be sure to tell them you respect them, above all else—and that you can keep your pulse on what's going on without restricting them from participation in what are the social phenomena of our day.

50

DON'T SWEAT THE SIBLING RIVALRY

✿ One of the most frustrating issues for moms of children of any age is having kids who cannot get along. It doesn't mean you have done anything wrong as a parent, but it hurts to see the children we love so much pick on or taunt one another, or be cruel. It's hard, then, for us to believe that fights between siblings can be either normal or healthy— but they are.

When we have a second child, we hold the fantastical vision that our older child will have a playmate (and a lifelong friend), when in reality, from the time they learn the word "mine," they are fighting for what belongs to them, materially and emotionally. The classic book in this area, *Siblings Without Rivalry* by Adele Faber and Elaine Mazlish, offers many wonderful tools for dealing with what is usually a fractious but short-lived period of time. They point out what I came to know: Eventually siblings do stop quarreling, or at least learn how to work through their differences.

As any of us with sisters or brothers recognize, there are many benefits to having siblings. Conflict resolution is often learned through the battles your kids have with one another. It helps them to establish who they are in the world and how to negotiate what they want. When children get older and are strongly differentiated from one another—when their differences in age, gender, extracurricular interests, or areas they excel in become expressed—you will find that rivalry lessens because their position and role in the family becomes clearer, especially to them. While each of them establishes their identity, they cease competing with one another to find the strengths and gifts that define them as unique and special. But it can take a while to get there, and you have to be the one handing out equal kudos to each child to help them individuate without jealousy.

Like all siblings, my girls, Jazz and Kenna, would alternate between being best friends and the most calculating opponents. It took time for each of them to become the strong girls and women they are, which in turn quelled their feelings of competition. When they were younger, I was invariably drawn into their struggles, but I learned that the role of peacemaker holds no glory. Often, I made things worse altogether. I discovered that three's a crowd in family conflict resolution, as one child invariably feels ganged up on and unsupported. Eventually, I insisted that the girls work out their own differences, realizing that if I didn't step out, they would always be coming to me.

So I worked with my girls when they were young to find a way to return to a peaceful resolution. I taught each of them how to listen with empathy to what the other had to say. I allowed them each to respond and to explain themselves in a back-and-forth manner. Sometimes, we'd take turns holding an object, like a glass heart, to identify the speaker. And then I asked them to come up with some possible solutions to their problem. We'd write these down, and the girls would decide on one. We'd revisit that a few hours, or days, later to see how it was working out. And if we had to, we'd look for another compromise. This approach established a foundation for resolving differences that evolved and deepened over the years.

Life is about problem-solving. Resolving sibling discord teaches important life skills and lessons about fairness, respect for others, self-control, and negotiation. It's important to understand that, while our children grow up in the same home, each of them experiences the world differently. They interpret the world through their own individual filter, just as adults do, and all events are seen through our own eyes. As parents, we can help them best when we encourage them to see their individual gifts and unique talents, and as they begin to grasp a sense of their identity, separate from their siblings and even from us, the rivalry will get easier. It also helps not to compare one child to the other one; that creates resentment.

I always tried to make my girls feel they were loved equally and celebrated uniquely. As they became more comfortable and confident in their own identities, winning, losing, or having their own way became less important. Don't sweat the sibling rivalry. It really does get better in time. And as your kids learn the skills to work out their issues, it is going to be the best communication training they ever have, and will ultimately serve them well.

51

PULL OFF TO THE SIDE OF THE ROAD

As our children grow and navigate their way through the scholastic and social journey of school, the amount of time we actually spend with them becomes very limited, especially if they are involved in extracurricular activities. As a matter of fact, you're lucky to get quality conversation time with him once your child has his own driver's license. Happily, our tweens and younger children still need us, and our "drive time" with them becomes ever more precious.

If you are like me, you may sometimes feel a little bit like Moses preparing the Children of Israel for the Promised Land, a place where he could not accompany them. Adulthood is like that, and so is life with a teenage driver. So I kept an ongoing list of concerns and objectives to go over with my kids, recognizing that as they grew older and their activities rolled together one right after the other, back-to-back, sometimes the only time I would really see them was first thing in the morning. Often, in our morning rush to get off to school, what should have been easy, early morning chatter quickly deteriorated into an argument, leaving bad feelings between us as we started the day.

I was speaking to a friend recently, and she admitted that she too sometimes forgets that the morning time she spends in the car with her oldest son, after dropping his little brother off for first grade, is sometimes the only one-on-one time she has with him, now that his afternoons are spent tutoring other children or in after-school sports programs.

As moms, we are often caught up in all the things that are on our lists to discuss with our children, and we look for the right moments to initiate those conversations. But what may be the right time for us may not be the perfect time for our child, captive audience though she may be in the passenger seat. We may erupt with our ideas and advice and reminders, but forget that our child may be doing her own mental preparation for the day, and that her agenda or priority list may be entirely different than ours.

One day my friend Julia shared such a story with me. She was rambling on in the car about the ten things that Sammy had to do after school when she glanced at him and noticed his expression. He was tapping his finger on his knee and frankly looked overwhelmed. "God, Mom, I feel like you just told me all the things I haven't done yet today, and I just woke up. My day has only started and already I have a stomachache. Can we just listen to the radio or something?"

Julia caught herself. She really didn't want to start the day on the wrong foot with an argument. So she did a very wise thing. She pulled off the road, even though this meant Sammy might be late for school.

She smiled, looked into his eyes, and reached over to give him a squeeze. She asked him to explain to her what part of that conversation bothered him, and then they discussed it. When she was satisfied that the feelings between them had shifted, and he felt better (and she felt better, too), she pulled back onto the road and into the drop-off lane. All they needed was three minutes to make things between them right again. Sammy smiled and gave her an unusual hug as he said, "I love you, Mom. See you after basketball tonight!" And, they were both back on track for a better day. It's up to us, as moms, not to forget how important it is to show our support for our kids, but we can do that more effectively by knowing when the best time is to communicate our list of what "to do" today.

52

THE GIFT OF BELONGING

✿ For those of us who remember family-oriented television like *The Waltons* and *Family Ties*, and other shows that emphasized strong family bonds, there is something wistful about how programming—and our world—has changed. Yet as demographics have shifted and new family structures have emerged, strong family bonds still sustain us. Perhaps more than ever, our youth need the strong value and support systems that come from family and community. The feeling of belonging keeps them safe. It prevents our kids from joining gangs and cliques that can hurt them, where unhealthy choices are made, and where lives can tip in the wrong direction.

The greatest blessing you can give your children is a sense of "belonging" to their clan of blood relatives. Our sense of family increases as we continue to share bonding times that include extended family: grandparents, aunts, uncles, and cousins. As you participate in and carry on family traditions with parties and reunions celebrating momentous occasions, your kids get to see what stuff they are made from, and are given the opportunity to know their heritage, which ultimately strengthens them as individuals.

The family unit structure is strengthened through spending time together. In addition, you can enhance that sense by guiding your children into activities with a greater community of like-minded supporters. Your church may have a youth group; your community may have organized sports and recreation leagues. These are areas outside the family that create community for our child, but still reflect our values and goals.

There is nothing like family dinners. I have a friend whose extended family has faithfully enjoyed Monday night dinners together for nearly twenty-five years—aunts, uncles, cousins, and grandparents. When the older children are away at college or the younger ones have a conflict, they are excused; otherwise, the entire family is expected to gather. It's where they want to be. For most of us, sitting down together to enjoy a meal is one of the most ancient traditions alive, and the place where family bonding occurs. Find the time to sit down together as often as you can. Have family members help to prepare the meal and to set and clear the table. Give a prayer of gratitude and thanksgiving while holding hands around the table. Take turns in lighthearted, easy banter around the table, and share the stories of the day. Discuss current events and world issues together. Acknowledge the joy but also the sorrows by checking in with each person: "How's your heart today?" This ensures that your kids know that no matter how their day went, or how much drama they are having with friends, they belong to a family where the love that holds them transcends anything negative that happens.

Go on family hikes. Go for picnics. Take in the scenery and fresh air of the outdoors. Think about road trips and visits to national landmarks. Go the beach, or to a national park. Camping experiences are among the most powerful ways to bond as a family. Getting back to nature and its simplicity is nourishing to a family's spirit. Campfires, roasted marshmallows, and nighttime stories told beneath a star-filled night sky make memories that create belonging. So do the rituals you perform at holiday time, on birthdays and anniversaries, and for special occasions. The more ritual and tradition you have, the greater connection to the family.

Take your time with your family. Slow down. Visit your extended family and go to weddings and funerals. Enjoy your holidays and create rituals that come through family traditions that are passed down through each generation. Create memories. When your kids know where they belong, they will always find their way home. Listen. Love. Share. Belong together. These bonds are forever.

53

THINK OF YOURSELF
AS THE CONTAINER

When you are carrying a child through pregnancy, you are the ultimate container. Wrapped in warmth and snuggled tight in your womb, your baby is safe, nurtured, and cared for. It is truly a miracle that our bodies create space to grow another human being within.

But we cannot always protect them once they leave our bodies. Childhood and adolescence can be bruising. Even the happiest, most expressive children can turn into depressed and unhappy teens and adults. Like water boiling in a kettle, their feelings must be safely vented. We can help our children avoid dangerous and self-destructive alternatives. Here's a strategy that you can implement to help your teens to express feelings that, left inside, will be repressed.

When Richard died, my dear friend, Challenge Day founder Yvonne St. John-Dutra, taught me to think of myself as the container that held space for my daughters' emotional expression as they went through their grief. Both of the girls were in high school, a dangerous time, when unhappy kids bottle up their feelings. Yvonne taught me to allow the girls to let their feelings out, and not to take their frustration, anger, and outrage personally. She taught me to think, instead, of holding their space as an empty container into which they could pour those feelings, releasing them safely, in a way that wouldn't hurt them. While I held their space, I didn't hold on to their emotions. As they released them, I did, too, allowing them to roll in and out like the tides.

High school is hard enough these days, but incorporating loss into the program adds a whole other dimension. There are many setbacks in life, and our kids experience many layers of loss. They may be going through a breakup, or having trouble with a teacher they don't like; they may feel out of place and alone at school, or feel overwhelmed with academic pressures. Whatever is driving their pain, this strategy will empower you to help them so they don't act out or turn their emotions into self-destructive behavior.

Kenna was just fourteen, and Richard's death shook her deeply. She couldn't eat, couldn't sleep; she cried and cried. This went on. I had to learn to hold her space while she let her feelings out. Yvonne taught me to ask the question "What else?" when Kenna would talk or be in a wave of grief. When someone is emptying, it makes a big difference if you can help them stay in that place a little longer and empty a little more. Sometimes, getting back to real peace means allowing the storm to build to a crescendo. Comforting someone out of their pain is not always the answer; asking "What else?" helps your child to find the place where there is energy that needs to be fully expressed, and they do this using their words, anger, and tears. It's like following a thread into the heart that needs mending.

Emotions are meant to be emoted. We cannot, nor should we, contain our tears any more than we can stifle our laughter. We've all seen how small children can cry and scream one moment, then laugh and giggle the next. They intuitively know to let go of their previous feelings. And so it is with the rest of us. We are all meant to move through our feelings, not sit in them. When we wallow in a negative environment, we are inviting the wound to fester. Infection inevitably follows.

As parents, you can't fix feelings, but you can make it safe for your children to have them. Think of yourself as your mother's arms around your child, holding him or her as if they were wrapped up tight in your belly again. As you learn to hold space for your child when they are expressing their emotions, you become, once again, the safe, nurturing place for them to land.

54

ADJUSTING YOUR GAME PLAN

❀ Over our lifetimes, and those of our parents, we have seen society change in dramatic ways. Technology and affluence have altered our standard of living and our vision of a good life—the life we want to give our children. As cities sprawled and many of us commuted to work by car, we may have traded up from owning one car to needing two. By the same token, we also learned that success means that you buy and trade up—just because you can. Our cultural standards have shifted from those of need to want; and our lives have become full of stuff we don't really need and cannot really afford.

We are living through one of the most challenging economic times since the Great Depression. Virtually no one has been untouched by the turbulence of the last few years. While levels of difficulty vary, we know that homelessness has risen along with joblessness; that food banks' shelves have thinned; and that in our own communities, services have been cut, while some of our neighbors are experiencing real hardship. We don't have to look beyond our own local streets to see the "For Sale" signs posted on lawns in our community.

I was at the supermarket the other day when I ran into a woman I have known for years. Her husband is an electrical contractor who has owned a successful business for two decades, but these last three years have been different. When his business was thriving, he and his wife bought a mountain cabin and overextended themselves, believing that everything would just continue as it was. And, *bam!* As building and remodeling came to a standstill, their expenses did not. It now appears that he will lose not only the mountain cabin, but also the family home, too. Sally teared up as she told me her news, and it just seemed so unfair to me, and I felt deep empathy for this family that had worked hard for their property. I realized with foreboding dread that this was a sign of the times.

While I know many friends are taking their losses on short sales and walking away from their homes to become renters, surprisingly, some are not devastated by their loss. They are looking at this as a time to put their lives into new order. They are grateful to have jobs and income, and are looking ahead to shifting into a simpler lifestyle that will allow them to better manage their monthly expenses. There is a relief in freeing ourselves from having to maintain a façade that we can no longer afford.

We can also find silver linings for our families in our downsized lives. We are showing our children the importance of flexibility, and how we adjust our circumstances to meet new realities. This is the story of life itself. It isn't always fair, and so much of what happens to us is out of our control. Families will often draw closer as they go on to successfully rebuild their lives. Kids may need to pick up a summer job earning extra money, learning to be more responsible, while contributing to their own financial needs. Many families have used their loss to strengthen the bonds of love. Others, who dwell in resentment and blame for having to let go of their material possessions, may fall apart. At what price do we want to hold on to the things that we can't take with us, anyway?

There is always a hidden gift in what may appear to be a catastrophic event. While letting go of a home is by no means easy, there are far greater losses. As a door closes, there is always an opportunity to open a new one. When we can bring our families closer together and return to a simpler, more independent and sustainable way of life, then we will not only survive, but also thrive.

55

EVERY FAMILY CAN GO "GREEN"

✿ I hate to admit it, but I really don't know much when it comes to the "green" movement. Still, I have recently focused my attention on understanding the small things I can do to decrease the size of my personal environmental footprint on our planet. I believe we should all feel responsible for helping Mother Earth make it to the next millennium. I spoke to my friend, author Sherry Ackerman, about living a sustainable life and about practical ideas for doing so as a family. Sherry's book, *The Good Life*, teaches the style of self-sustainable living she follows in her own life. I asked her to make some suggestions that would help every family go green together:

- Have your children color, paint, or collage durable, strong-handled, brown paper grocery bags in order to turn them into reusable bags for trips to the supermarket. Each child can have his or her own special grocery bag to use. The nickel credit that some stores give to shoppers for bringing their own bag can go to the child.

Your son or daughter can then put each nickel into a savings program and begin to learn about balancing saving and spending.

- Have older children help wash the dinner dishes. Teach water conservation by inserting dishpans into the sink bays that, after the dishes have been done (with eco-friendly, biodegradable detergent, of course), can be carefully carried outside to water outdoor plants. Discuss how many gallons of water are being saved by re-using the dishwater. Raise awareness of water as "the next oil."

- Create a winter sewing project where children are given scraps of brightly colored cloth from which to make cloth vegetable bags. (Many thrift stores give unsold clothing away, and these items can be salvaged for cloth for this kind of project.) Each bag can be a different size and secured with a simple drawstring at the top. Then, when going to the grocery store, they can be dampened (especially in the summer) and used to bring home vegetables. The damp cloth bag keeps the vegetables crisp—and eliminates the need for plastic bagging. This activity will give you an opportunity to introduce the problems associated with plastic bag overuse and disposal.

- Plan an outing to a farm involved in community-supported agriculture. Find out how local food is produced and distributed. Talk to the produce personnel to find out what fruits and vegetables grow best in your area. What does "eating local" mean? Most local farms that serve metropolitan areas welcome visitors, especially children, and many have plenty of safe farm animals for petting: goats, cows, and horses.

- Start a Sustainability Circle youth group. The group can offer readings, films, outings, and hands-on projects about different aspects of sustainability. Once the group members are up to speed on pressing sustainability issues, they can sponsor local workshops where families come and learn how (and why) to reduce waste, conserve, and reuse.

- Teenage girls love playing fashion designer. Take them to a local thrift store and let them select a number of different items that they will bring home and "make over" into their own special fashions. You will be surprised at their creativity and innovativeness. Some of the new looks that come out of a project like this are really sassy! And the girls will appreciate that even clothing may be recycled and repurposed.

- Do trash audits together. Trash audits are conducted by dumping the contents of the household trash onto a tarp and, using rubber gloves, carefully picking through in order to identify things that can be recycled. Separate out paper, cardboard, plastic, aluminum, and glass—all of which are recyclable. Also separate out any food scraps, since they can be used in garden compost. This exercise will surprise you, as you will have very little trash left after you have separated out the recyclables. Do the exercise together as a family, and talk about it. Discuss ways to make recycling a habit.

- Have a Vegetarian Night at least once a week. Experiment with new, vegetarian recipes. Start with guaranteed winners like vegetarian pizza and spinach lasagna. Include children in the food preparation, and talk about the positive ecological impact of eating "lower on the food chain."
- Declare a moratorium on the clothes dryer for the summer. Put up a clothesline and get a bucket of old-fashioned wooden clothespins. Have the kids help hang out the laundry on sunny days. Enjoy the smell of fresh, air-dried sheets and towels. A practical piece of wisdom passed down from Sherry's grandmother is to leave your white linens out all night during full moons and take advantage of how lunar light actually whitens them without chemical bleaches or commercial products. Use this to teach children about the power of nature. Brainstorm together to identify other ways you can use nature's gifts to replace toxic, chemical processes.

56

BEING A "COOL" MOM ISN'T
WHAT YOUR CHILD NEEDS

✿ I've seen my share of mothers over the years that make the mistake of wanting to be "friends" with their kids before their parenting role is done. Your children already have friends—their contemporaries. What they need is for you to parent them, shaping their behavior with the purposefulness only an adult can give. This means that we have to put off friendship with our children until a later date. Being the "cool" mom who acts more like a friend does not give you authority when you need it, and you must be able to set and uphold the rules of your household.

When Jasmine was very little, she asked me if I was her friend. I replied, "I love you differently than your friends do. I love you so much that I need to teach you what's right and wrong, and give you consequences if you need them. I need you to listen to me and trust that I know certain things that you can't know yet about how to keep yourself safe from harm. Your friends don't give you those things, do they?" She nodded and said, "No, Mommy, my friends don't do those things. You're better than having a best friend because you love me so much."

You can see the moms that struggle with wanting friendship from their teens too early. They do things like provide alcohol at parties, and they party with their underage kids. They don't impose curfews at night. They don't really know what's going on in school, because they take everything their kids say to them at face value. They never say "no."

It's a tough balance, because we want to maintain rapport with our kids. We want a peaceful, happy home. And the tween and teen years are hard enough. No one wants an angry, sullen teen who shrieks and tells you you're ruining their life. On the other hand, when you impose limits and remind your child that you are not peers, that he or she does not have an equal say in how something gets decided, you are giving your child a gift. Whether they understand it now or not, your guidance is their friend. The time to be friends with your children will come later, when they are grown and out of your house, making their own rules and suffering their own consequences. Until then, they have plenty of friends.

Lori is the mother of Toren, who is eleven. He was scheduled to attend a birthday party after school and carpool with one of his friends' parents. At some point the plan changed, and Toren mentioned that the mom in charge of driving them to the party had given them the public transportation schedule and bus fare instead. When Lori heard about this she said flat out, "No! You aren't riding the bus to the party!"

As Lori related this story to me, she reflected sadly that she wished she could be more "cool" in her son's eyes. She was afraid she was losing her connection to him. I responded, "Actually, your son doesn't need a cool mom. He just needs to know why you don't think it's in his best interest to take the bus." I suggested to her that being "cool" doesn't necessarily mean that she has to automatically agree with whatever her child wants to do or presents her with, but rather, she might consider using a different approach. Instead of just issuing a blanket "no" without explanation, she could sit down with him and discuss the bus as an option, but also talk about her concerns about his safety. Looking at the situation together in an effort to build rapport, but making and sticking with the decision you are comfortable with, is as "cool" as I think it needs to get.

Family life is not a democracy, and you are the chief executive. You need to have authority as a parent so that the boundaries you set are observed and respected. Your kids need you to lead the way, and being too "cool" puts you on equal ground when you really need to be a step up. There is a time for everything, and when the time is right, even though you'll always be their mother, you will turn into the best of friends.

57

GO AHEAD AND HAVE A GOOD CRY

✿ One thing I know to be true: Being a happy person does not mean that you are happy all the time. My measure of happiness is not about feeling exuberant joy every minute of every day; it is measured by how quickly I bounce back from the lows, and how gracefully I move through the small and the big stuff of life. Happiness is a perspective, not a pursuit.

We have heard many times that it is in the journey, the process, and not the destination through which one finds fulfillment. Sometimes the twists and turns that are a natural part of the path require our perseverance and test our strength. I have come to realize that resiliency is the most important quality in living a truly joy-filled life. What that means is allowing yourself to experience the emotional responses you have in the moment, to a situation or to an ongoing problem, without repression, and allowing yourself the liberty to express whatever you feel inside. When you do, you will be buoyant and truly resilient.

Life is a big experience and holds in it many blessings. But things also happen to us that we don't choose, but which nevertheless become part of our process. We are challenged; we are in pain; we are frustrated and feel powerless. It is part of the human experience, but it can feel isolating and overwhelming.

I used to find it very difficult to give myself permission to cry. I would feel sad and know that I needed to cry, but I would distract myself instead. We all find our ways of dealing with such heartache and low moods, and some of them are not at all the healthiest means. As one friend who was experiencing marriage problems and a particularly bad patch with a teenage daughter would tell me, what was getting her through her toughest days as she numbed out to her sad feelings was her retail therapy.

In my professional life I have had the opportunity to serve on the board of directors and Global Leadership Council of Challenge Day, an organization whose mission is to make every child on the planet feel safe, loved, and celebrated. Children participate in workshops, doing "heart work," where volunteers are helped to renegotiate their emotional training and add a few tools to their emotional tool belts. One of the main things participants are taught by Challenge Day leaders is that it is healthy to cry. Crying releases the toxic emotions and allows our bodies to quiet and to refresh and replenish, much as sleep does. We can't fight sleep, just as we cannot contain pain and frustration. We need to release it.

This same lesson applies to parents. During a workshop I attended, I noticed how easily my friend Yvonne could cry almost on cue, whereas I would fight it the way a toddler who doesn't want to go to bed will fight sleep. Then she and I partnered during an exercise where each of us drew a word from a hat and had fifteen minutes to model that word to the group. Yvonne laughed when I drew the word "vulnerable." When it was my turn, I grabbed her hands and pulled her to the center of the room. I held Yvonne's hands and asked her show me "vulnerable" while I committed myself to mirroring her response. Our eyes locked and I stayed there as she searched my soul and then we cried tears together, my first tears in many years.

I have learned that happiness is within myself and that I can always tap into it, as you too can. We can do this when we give ourselves complete permission to accept our feelings, even our low moods and negative thoughts, as they are. I can assure you that I have them almost every day. But instead of denying those feelings, I choose to notice them, to allow them to wash in and through me. When I sit with my feelings in nonresistance and allow them to come forward, the feelings inevitably subside like dust in the wind. The moment is over. Crying is a friend to moms, because it lets out in small doses the frustrations and feelings that need to be released so that you can continue to give all that you do so selflessly.

I have found that giving myself permission to cry and to even have an occasional meltdown is the quickest way to clear confusion and re-align with my center. Incredibly, tears are healing, and honoring your emotions allows you to feel your life.

I am envious when I hear a woman say, "I cry so easily." As a mom, I would encourage you to now and then have a good cry. Some days, you may have something to cry about. On others, you may not know why you feel low. When you do, stay with your feelings, and don't distract yourself from them. As you move through them and release your tears and quiet down again, you will feel as if you have had a cathartic cleanse. It's not a weakness to cry. In fact, your tears will lead the way to discovering your inner reserves of courage and wisdom. Be graceful when you're low and grateful when you're high, and remember "This too shall pass," as your tears will always return you to happier days.

58

HOW MUCH TV, INTERNET, AND VIDEO GAMES ARE TOO MUCH?

❋ We live in a world of new media that grows and changes by the minute. Our kids navigate it with an ease that makes us feel our age. Yet, some things haven't changed very much; we know that television, while an important educational tool, can also project negative stereotypes and values that are inconsistent with our own. Left to their own devices, our children will watch entirely too much TV. In addition, the Internet, cable (offering hundreds of channels, some of them with decidedly adult content), and video games, with their sometimes violent imagery, mean that you'll want to exercise a level of scrutiny that would have been un-necessary during our own childhoods.

We also know that TV, the Internet, and video games are an instant form of gratification and entertainment, which is why they can become so addictive. We need to be mindful about how much time our kids spend involved in these activities, and to consider at what cost. Obviously, the more time they spend glued to a tech-box, the less time they are spending creatively playing outdoors the old-fashioned way, or reading or doing homework or just plain dreaming. We also know that kids can lack focus because of the distractions, or that the distractions themselves can be quite questionable.

For all these reasons, parents need to think about ways to control the time and manner in which their children engage in these activities, and to put parental controls in place to help their kids avoid the pitfalls of the interactive world. Here are some ways:

1. Keep your computer in a central place in your home so that you can cruise by and look over your child's shoulder. Keep the TV out of his bedroom; your child will watch less and, as with the computer, you'll have a greater chance of monitoring what he does view.

2. Spend time teaching your kids how to use the Internet safely and appropriately.

3. Check the history component available in the menu of your computer's browser. It is important to know what sites your kids are cruising.

4. Use privacy settings and sharing controls available on social networking sites.

5. Teach your children about Internet predators, and that you can't trust someone to be who they say they are. Anyone can make up an alias. Your children should never post their real name, age, school, or address on social networking sites.

6. Teach your kids responsible communication. If you wouldn't say it to someone's face, don't write it online. Tell your teens that Facebook pages should never contain visual or written content that could embarrass them. Prospective employers and college admission officers have been known to check the Facebook pages of applicants.

7. Use your parental controls for TV programming. If your TV was purchased after January 2000, it has technology that allows you to block programs you don't want your children exposed to (this is also true of digital or cable TV). These are accessed through your television's remote control. Consult the instruction manual or call your service provider to learn how to eliminate certain adult channels.

8. When you buy a new video game, check it out by playing it first.

9. Determine boundaries for usage. ("You may use the Internet or play video games after your homework is complete, but only for one hour.")

10. It's harder to track or supervise the habits of older children, who may have mobile devices such as smartphones or laptop computers. Tracking software exists that allows you to be sure they are visiting appropriate sites, but be sure they know you will be checking up on them periodically. You don't want to violate their privacy, or for them to feel you believe they cannot be trusted. Honesty is as important as safety.

Television is a powerful medium that has an intense ability to reach and influence its viewers—adults and children alike. The images portrayed often shape the values of our culture. In my research for this book, I viewed Jennifer Siebel Newsom's documentary *Miss Representation*. In this film, she is inspired by becoming a mother herself and wondering what life will hold in opportunities for her daughter. She shows us many of the negative impacts of television, and how reality-based programming is creating stereotypes that make it difficult for young women to break the mold of these negative images, and the negative impact on their perceived roles and choices for their future. It's a very informative film, and reminded me that television is not regulated by any standards of excellence. Therefore, it is our responsibility as moms to check out the programs and how they may impact our kids.

Responsible parenting is using the controls you have so that your kids are not exposed to a world that they are not mature enough to understand. Keep in mind that the creators of most video games and television shows don't keep your child's best interest in mind when building their product. As an empowered parent, don't give up your right to control what influences your child. Restrictions may make them upset with you now, but they'll love you for it later.

59

YOUR KIDS WILL CALL YOU OUT

❀ If many of us were shown a video of what our lives would be like raising a family, we would say, "There's no way I can do all of that!" As a mother, though, you know that your life would be vastly different if you never had children. Raising a family presents us with a richness and a quality of life that would be difficult to attain if the world revolved solely around our own wants and desires. One could say that being a mother is a soul journey, and our children can teach us as much as we teach them.

Kids have, from a young age, a candor and no-nonsense way of telling it like it is, and for innocently calling us out on our flaws and missteps. My friend calls her son "the prosecutor"—if she's not getting to the gym, or he thinks she is working too hard, he'll tell her. There are times when she looks at him and thinks, *Who are you? Leave me alone and go be a kid.* It's very uncomfortable to be taken down by your own child. Yet she wouldn't have it any other way; sometimes, our kids provide us with just the right-timed, honest reflection we need.

When you embrace family life, your ego goes through a complete annihilation process. Your identity shifts dramatically, along with your lifestyle, as the circumstances of raising children change your life forever. My dad always said, "You are not truly an adult until you become a parent. Being responsible for another human being is what brings you into selfless adulthood." Motherhood is arguably the greatest and most profound transition you will ever make in your lifetime. You shift from an egocentric world where every decision revolves around you and only your spiritual, physical, and emotional needs into a new life where the claims and needs of another person will always come ahead of yours. For all the attention and intention we give them, our kids have a way of mirroring back to us all our strengths and our weaknesses, putting our patience, creativity, and problem-solving skills to the test every day.

There is a reflective quality, spiritually speaking, to the relationship we have with our children. When we interact, sometimes it is like holding up a magnifying glass to all our good stuff, and also to the stuff we'd rather not see. We often say that our kids have an ability to push our buttons, but we don't really understand what that means beyond superficial issues of patience and disagreement. When you think about it, however, there's a lot more going on. For instance, my kids just know how to get me when they are upset with something I say. I classically have poor timing when delivering an important message. At least, that's what they say. It has become my observation that if you want to make people mad, lie; if you want to make them absolutely livid, tell the truth. I will blurt out the truth as I see it, and it isn't always in the most subtle fashion. When I do this and they don't want to hear what I have to say, they will mention a hot spot to deflect the emphasis of the conversation off of them and onto me. All moms know that it is difficult and often painful to argue with someone who knows all your soft spots. One of my personal hot spots is when my kids call me out accusatorially: "Mom, you don't walk your talk."

Honestly, this hits my hot button almost as much as disrespect. If my kids are disrespectful, I see red and light up like a stick of dynamite. And when they question my authenticity, I have the same reaction. While disrespect is unacceptable, I can take a good look at the reflection in the mirror when they call me out on authentic expression. Let's face it, it's a whole lot easier to give advice than to live by everything you say—and it is one of the ways in which I am most hard on myself. I value authenticity above all else, and struggle with my inner critic all the time. So, of course, my kids are aware of this button to push. Like that CNN slogan about "keeping them honest," our kids do the same by calling our attention to those things we may not want to shine the light on so brightly.

If you can see your child as your teacher in this way, it can really facilitate your personal growth. The ultimate way to take personal responsibility for your reactions and responses to life is to ask yourself why it is that something hits your hot spot. The biggest lesson I have learned as a mother is humility. Children will always call you out and keep you humble, and your hot spots will tell you where you need to cool off. While it is socially our task to nourish and offer them insight and wisdom for growth, don't lose the opportunity to learn from your children as they call you out, offering the truest mirror of yourself.

60

SLOW DOWN AND WAKE UP
TO YOUR LIFE

The reality of our lives is that we fill them. We fill every inch of our schedules with activity. We participate in sports, attend committee meetings, and visit the orthodontist and pediatrician. Then there are trips to the library, car pools, religious school, practice time, and a myriad of social appointments—which are squeezed in between hours of homework (yes, I'm just talking about the kids here!). Once the kids move beyond elementary school, you can forget family dinners. For years, our family calendar looked like a complex science project, with every white space filled with a color-coded road map highlighting appointments. Jazzy was pink; Kenna was blue; Richard, yellow; and me, orange. We moved along the fast track this way through the middle school and high school years, knowing it was insane, feeling the stress of our lives, but not knowing how to step off the treadmill. Everything new that was possible seemed like an opportunity too good to pass up, and our kids always seemed to rally on to the next level in everything they did. For all intents and purposes, we appeared to be a family that could get it all done and still create some balance, too. Yet deep down, we knew that something about this lifestyle wasn't right for us. It was just too fast.

Then, one day as I was finishing some Christmas shopping, I pulled into a mall parking space and I received the phone call that shattered our lives. My Richard was gone. This was the day that we slowed down to the speed of life.

When the time came to pick up our old routines as best we were able, I did what I could to restore some order in the girls' lives. One way I did this was by lightening their academic loads. I took Kenna off the advanced academic track and replaced that with a gentler schedule, allowing her more rest. Jazz had only a semester left until she graduated high school; by that point, there wasn't much I could do for her, but her teachers did all they could to assist her.

As my heart broke open, I became aware of how numb to my feelings the crazy chop-chop schedule we had maintained had made me. I realized that I had jumped on the bandwagon of fear of "not keeping up." I was holding life as if it were a tightly strung box, and I was caught up in my roles of wife and mother. I was living under the illusion that I could control life. One of the great understandings I came to in that first year of grief was that, in my pain and suffering, I was feeling life with a new level of awareness. I was awake and hadn't known I was asleep. By doing less, I was taking in, and appreciating, so much more.

As life slowed, I began to engage in every moment with the complete presence that practicing stillness and living in your heart brings. As I healed from my loss, grief taught me that beyond the portal of sorrow lies the portal to a simpler kind of joy and love. My scrambled routine quieted. I listened now to my emotions in ways I never had. I found joy in the presence of simplicity, and magic in the moment.

We had been caught up in a lifestyle that left us exhausted, with little time to spend as a family. Now, it was too late to get that time back. However, I learned that, as Norman Cousins so poignantly observed, "The tragedy of life is not death but what we let die inside us while we live." I learned through loss how important it is to take charge of our busy lives. This time we spend together is short, and doing more isn't always the answer. Perhaps there's room in the schedule for some white space where we can fill in the blanks with presence.

61

LISTEN TO ME

✻ If you ask almost any teenager what they most want from their parents, they will likely say, "I want to be heard." And, ironically, if you ask parents what they would like most from their teens, they will say, "I wish my kids would just listen to me." I can't tell you how many times my girls felt frustrated that I wasn't hearing them, and I felt the same frustration. Sometimes it is as though there is a wall separating parents and children. We get locked in our own reactive thoughts that spin through our heads, and are unable to listen.

I was speaking with my friend's daughter Liza, a high school junior, not long ago. I asked her, "What do you think makes a really good mom?" She responded, "My mom is at her best when she just hears me out. Most of the time when I come to her with my problems, I just want someone to listen." My friend Nancy sets a great example in her parenting because she remembers what it was like to be a teen herself. It is truly important to try to see the world through our children's eyes, a world in which so much has changed, and where so much about growing up remains the same. They still have so much to learn through experience and, hard as it is for us to stand by, we need to understand that our best advice will be given only when we are asked for it. Oftentimes, kids need only to know their parents can relate to what they are going through, and affirm their experience with empathy. Sometimes, words—our words—just don't help, and other times, our words are heard with open ears.

Richard was always a better listener than I was. Many times, I wished I had done things differently, and still at times I lack the compassion necessary to be a truly responsive listener. When Kenna was adjusting to her new school, as I've written, it wasn't an easy transition. There were many afternoons when she would come home from school and just cry and cry. I often wonder if I had been better at listening and able to just be a container for her feelings, if she would have adjusted faster. Looking back, I remember feeling irritated and impatient because she couldn't seem to understand we were going to great lengths to give her the education she deserved. Kids, after all, see things from their own vantage point. I was making a critical error by wishing she would see it my way.

The irony is that being a responsive listener often means you just hold space for your child—that is, you don't try to make it better; you don't try to insert your ideas and experience into the matter. You just let your child experience his or her feelings, and you listen. Richard had a way of sitting like Buddha and nodding his head or holding the girls in his arms as they cried. I, on the other hand, was more of a reactive listener. My concern and involvement in their lives was so great that I couldn't stand helplessly by (or so I thought). I felt that if something was wrong, it was somehow because of something I had done, or failed to do. And so I felt it was up to me to step in. All I wanted was for them to be happy. And so, like many well-meaning moms, I talked, and talked, and sometimes, I'm sure, all that talking made things worse.

I have learned through much failure and a few successes that there are just two ways to respond when your children come to you with their problems about school, friendships, and ethics and values. Whether you are talking about child issues such as "Mommy, I don't like it that Sally gets more playing time than me. It's not fair" or adult issues such as "Mom, I want to get on birth control," you can react from fear, taking what they say personally, or you can respond from love, offering empathy and support. When we react fearfully to what they say, it is often because we are placing our feelings first: We think, *How will this impact my life? Will I be embarrassed in front of my friends? This isn't how I raised you.* Most times, kids just need to vent their feelings. Other times, they are asking for real guidance.

The alternative to reacting from fear is staying present in a nonjudgmental way as your children share their concerns and stories, taking in what they say and listening empathetically to the feelings behind the words. As we become great listeners, we can build the trust and respect we need by hearing them first and meeting in a place of love, heart to heart, so that when the time comes and it matters most, they will also hear what we have to say.

62

CHANGE IT UP

✾ I learned a long time ago that kids thrive with structure, but that your daily routine can leave you in a slump, and a rut. If you want to rejuvenate your energy, you have to change it up. If your health is good but you still experience symptoms of fatigue, lack of interest, and feeling you have the doldrums, these are strong indicators you need to shift gears. Small, incremental changes can yield big results in your attitude. Feeling positive again and recovering your passion for living can spill over into all areas of your life, especially adding joy to your parenting. When you insert something new into your day, even the most rote and mundane daily tasks, such as packing those lunches or folding laundry, can feel more tolerable. Routine is important, but variety is the spice of life.

Here are some small changes you can make that can help you shift internally, so you feel less tired emotionally and more inspired:

- A few decades ago, a survey of women revealed that when they were feeling a little low and in a rut, buying a new lipstick would give them a lift. It seems so simple, but it doesn't really take much to raise your spirits. Everyone likes a treat now and then. Think about downloading some new tunes on your iPod, or treating yourself to a new CD. Do something nice for yourself. Change it up: If you mostly read nonfiction, consider reading fiction, and vice versa.

- Start your day with a new meditation or inspirational reading. You can receive these daily on your computer or a smart phone. It's always important to make sure you schedule time for quiet reflection, even if you have to get up fifteen minutes earlier or stay up fifteen minutes later than usual. This will create a feeling of positive space in you that can increase your energy and help you overcome the monotony of your daily routine through new insight and inspiration.

- Spice it up in the kitchen: Instead of rushing to get dinner on the table, take your time so you can enjoy the preparation and presentation of the meal. The energy you put into it will nourish your entire family and make you feel good. Use weekends to get a head start. Go online and plan a menu. Often, we get into food ruts, too. The morning shows, food magazines, and food networks all have Web sites chock-full with new ideas. Be adventurous, but also try to make healthy choices.

- It's amazing what creatures of habit we are. We drive to many of the same places every day and we always choose the same route. Altering your driving routes to school, to work, or when you run errands can often bring new awareness and perk up your drive time. It's a good metaphor to show your kids that there is more than one way to get somewhere, just like there is more than one way to solve a problem.

- Try a new exercise class or add a weekly hike to your health regime, and consider making it social by doing it with friends. Start a new hobby or make time to pursue an interest such as photography, painting, writing poetry, or scrapbooking.

- Pursue a dream you've had on the back burner by making incremental small steps each week. Maybe you've always wanted to write a children's story or you have an inventive idea. Make a plan to move in a new direction by taking action steps to spring your dream forward into reality.

- Participate in a community service event or project, or choose a new organization to donate free time to. There are small jobs and larger ones that nonprofit organizations need volunteers to help with.

- Spend more time in nature. Get your hands dirty in the garden.

- Do a creative project in arts and crafts, or home remodeling or repair.

- Write a letter to your kids that shares what you would say to them in your last hour of life. It always helps us to live with higher appreciation when we realize that things can change suddenly.

- Make a list of ten things you wish you had time to do and work your way up from the bottom.

- Read a frivolous novel purely for entertainment or a book you can't put down.
- Shake up your personal style and try a new haircut. It doesn't just have to be about lipstick, you know. Get a manicure or a pedicure and choose a crazy new nail color, or do both.
- Don't forget that you need your playtime. You need both date nights and time with your girlfriends. Your kids enjoy their play-dates and so should you.
- Change it up by adding a new class or visit a new park to play at. Getting out of the house together is a must, and having fun is, too!

While there is an inherent sweetness—not to mention ease—in the habits and routines we create, innovation and change keeps us eternally young, interested, and interesting to ourselves, as well as to others. Invention and new discoveries are some of life's great little pleasures. Don't be afraid to treat yourself.

63

MINIMIZE YOUR MAMA DRAMA

❋ One of the things I wasn't prepared for in raising girls was revisiting all the Mean Girl and Queen Bee "drama" I thought I had left behind in my own youth. Nothing rekindles your own unresolved feelings like watching your children go through similar and very painful experiences. During such times, it's important to remember to balance your innate desire to protect your children without crossing a line and becoming overinvolved in what should be their drama now, not yours.

It doesn't occur to us when we are new mothers that we will revisit those hurt feelings of our past hurts through our child. Somehow, we hoped our children would be immune from those experiences; we never would have anticipated that our lovely, perfect daughters would be whispered about by other girls, excluded from sleepovers, or suddenly dropped by their friends. It's so easy to feel personally attacked when your child is emotionally wounded by another child. It's easy to forget that kids will be kids, and that they learn through conflict and disappointment, even though in our minds we may see an act against our child as unfair, or even evil. What happens to our child happens to us, because we personalize it. How could we not? But when we do, we are as good as stepping into the drama ourselves, and we never make it better by stepping in. In fact, it's not our problem to heal.

I know a woman who learned this firsthand. Her twelve-year-old is in the thick of a Mean Girl drama. Sarah is generally a self-confident girl, but by Friday afternoon had finally been reduced to tears by her "friend" Allison's berating criticism. Sarah wasn't funny. Sarah was a terrible dancer. Sarah wasn't cool. Carly was cool. And Allison and Carly had now forged a fast friendship and it looked like Sarah was out. The next morning, however, while Sarah was sleeping, her phone buzzed with a text message. It was from Allison with yet another unkind remark. Sarah's mom couldn't resist, and she picked up the phone and began a text conversation with Allison while pretending to be her daughter. She couldn't stand the way Sarah's feelings were being hurt and thought she could toss off a few cutting remarks of her own that would put the girl in her place. Bad idea! She made the situation much worse because Allison figured out pretty quickly it wasn't Sarah she was texting with, but her mom. And when Monday came around, and an unknowing Sarah came in for teasing that was more brutal than ever, my friend realized that rather than empower Sarah to say the right things, she had taken matters into her own hands and made this her "mama drama."

The extent of our involvement with our girls and their friends, and the boundaries we set for ourselves, isn't always simple. Many of us have met some of our most lasting friends through our children. Maybe they met during the kinder, gentler time of preschool or early elementary school, when relationships between children were more homogenous. When every child was invited to every birthday party, played on the kickball team, and received a medal at the end of the season. But as our kids age, classes become tracked; bodies change, and so do interests. Some kids develop faster, both emotionally and physically. Not everyone makes the travel team, the cheerleading squad, becomes editor in chief of the yearbook, or has a boyfriend. That is to say, as our children age, they discover that their lives become more competitive.

As our children's lives change, sometimes women who met through their sons and daughters and became close friends find that their relationship has changed, too, simply because their children are no longer close and it's painful or awkward. Or sometimes two women can be close, but their sons or daughters who are the same age just don't like each other. These are all potential "mama dramas"—dramas that can be navigated when you agree to accept that that's how things are, and that each child is moving ahead with his or her life in the way that makes best sense for them. Sometimes it's enough to just tiptoe around the topic of each other's kids, silently understanding that you don't want your friend to feel bad about what's happening for your child and not hers, and to just focus on yourselves.

We moms are of course triggered emotionally by the things that happen to our kids that bring up issues from our own bruised childhoods. As I learned to see these emotional triggers with awareness and remind myself that I couldn't re-create my own emotional healing through my daughter's experience, then I remembered to stand behind her for support, but not to participate in her drama directly. I valued my friendships with other mothers and realized that we could all agree not to get involved. There is a fine line between resolving things for our kids and what they need to learn to do for themselves. I learned that it's best to minimize my own personal involvement in my kids' conflicts, maintain a watchful protective eye, and empower them by giving them the right words to speak, but keep the "mama dramas" to a minimum.

64

THE KEYS TO PARENTING
IN PARTNERSHIP

❀ Study after study shows that children flourish best when they are parented in a partnership. Whether married or no longer together, we do our best for our children when we give them the benefit of two parents who can find the common goal of working together.

Parenting as partners begins with understanding the different perspectives—life histories, traditions, and individual experiences—each of you brings to raising children. Our families of origin may have used completely different parenting styles. Sensitivity to these differences, rather than judgments, creates understanding and a capacity to find solutions you can both feel comfortable with. Besides that, there are a few keys that will really help you parent effectively with your spouse or co-parent, without the recurrent conflict and disagreement that undermine your children's best interests:

1. Be a united front: Never correct each other in front of your children because it diminishes and undermines the authority of the

other parent. If your partner or co-parent says or does something you don't agree with, speak privately when your children are not present. Work out your disagreements between you, even if you must agree to disagree, at times.

2. Acknowledge the good things your partner does instead of always pointing to the flaws.

3. Remind yourself that your co-parent loves your kids as much as you do.

4. Whether you share a household or not, be consistent in your discipline, using the same rules, consequences, and language.

5. Work together in establishing and executing your parenting strategies. Keep these conversations private.

6. Never speak to your children negatively about your co-parent or about your personal issues regarding that co-parent. Your kids should not carry the burdens of any negativity in your relationship with each other.

7. Openly applaud the other parent's good points.

8. Do your best, even if you are separated, to spend time together with your kids that is amicable and friendly.

9. Schedule weekly meetings to discuss the issues at hand so you can create an action plan together and keep communication between you open.

10. Identify each of your strengths and what you each bring to the table, and then use those strengths to create better lives for your children.

65

SAY IT WITH POST-ITS AND TEXTS

❀ Here's a tip that makes communicating with your kids easier. It really works, and is simplicity itself.

It's baffling to think of the power struggles that ensued with my girls, and their lack of response over what I thought of as simple requests or reminders of things they should do on their own. After several gentle attempts didn't work, I all but became a nag. At this point, my kids would build a wall of resistance just hearing the tone of my voice, and would tune me out. It didn't matter how many times I asked, my requests would fall on deaf ears. And, truthfully, I didn't enjoy repeating myself like a broken record (an analogy they don't understand) any more than they wanted to hear me.

In middle school, Jazz needed physical therapy for a shoulder injury. As part of her P.T., she had to do a series of rubber-band exercises, much like those swimmers do, to strengthen the muscles around her shoulders. At the time, she was still wearing braces, and also had to wear orthodontic rubber bands to bring her top and bottom jaws into alignment. She was twelve, and didn't understand the long-term consequences to her shoulders or teeth if she didn't follow through.

Kenna was a vegetarian, and needed to take vitamin supplements to balance out her diet. Her situation was easier to oversee because I could stand by the breakfast table and see if she took them. If I wasn't there, more often than not I'd find her breakfast eaten but the vitamins still beside her napkin.

Anything related to their health were nonnegotiable items in our house, so these issues with the girls turned into nagging sore spots between us. Richard was on a book tour and traveling when I called him one day in complete frustration that the girls wouldn't listen to me; there had to be some simpler way of communicating to inspire a different attitude that would help them follow through. He suggested that I write notes instead of giving them verbal reminders, to take the power struggle out of our communication. I went to the store and bought different colored Post-its and started putting them around their bedrooms, in the kitchen, and on the bathroom mirrors, where I knew they would notice them. They did. At first, they would post the read notes on the entry table by the front door as they left for school in the morning. The good news is, they worked. Eventually, each note was color-coded and edited down to a one-word reminder. I used blue for "Bands?" and pink for "Vitamins?" I even began using the notes for other reminders, too: "Feed dog," "Reading log," "Laundry away."

When the girls entered high school, their "to do" lists were more complex, but they were even less prone to listen to me. I have to admit, I wasn't thrilled with the amount of texting going on between the girls and their friends. The technology seemed so impersonal, and I also noticed that my kids weren't listening to my voice-mail messages any longer. If you want your kids to listen, you have to meet them on their turf and speak in their language. I came to realize that texting is how this generation communicates, and in order for me to get their attention, I needed to get with the program. Here, too, I found that taking the personal pressure out of the reminders (for both of us) and putting them in a text message actually worked well for all kinds of instructions. I have learned that I can say things to my kids on a Post-it note or in a text that would otherwise come off as just another lecture from Mom if I tried to deliver the same message in person. With the pressure off, from time to time, they even sought me out with a text. If they were having test anxiety, they often would text me to tell me they were scared. I would text them back, "BREATHE."

Texting cannot or should not replace face-to-face conversation about real issues, but there's no complaining or talking back in texting. It's a medium kids understand, although I try never to text my kids when they are in the car. Texting while driving is so dangerous.

Whether I want to convey information, a gentle reminder to remember about self-care, or just say, "I love you," texts and Post-it notes take the power struggle out of the interaction and give the control back to your child. They encourage personal responsibility and follow-through, and take far less energy on your part. Best of all, there is no more nagging.

66

GUILT-FREE WORKING MOM

❀ When you have a job or career outside the home that you are passionate about and you have a child who means more to you than life itself, your life is filled with conflicting impulses that can leave you feeling fragmented and guilty. There can be many emotions to reconcile as you navigate your professional life while always being a mom. Sometimes we work by choice because we have a passion for it; sometimes we work because we have no choice. And some of us work to give our families a quality of life they wouldn't have without it. Whether we work in home offices and hear our children outside our office door, or see them during the day when we take breaks, we may feel just as tormented as the mom who leaves the house early in the morning and returns many hours later. When we close a door on our child—any door—we feel they are losing something, and so are we.

We've all read the studies that remind us there are long-term benefits for children of working moms. We also know there are just as many benefits for children whose mothers stay at home. How you spend your hours—with or away from your child—should never be tagged by guilt or judgment on the part of others (let's all agree to put an end to those Mommy Wars). The thing is, wherever you are in your day, give your work the same 100 percent you would be giving the kids, and vice versa. When we don't honor that choice, we devalue the children for whom we make it. Our choices and decisions have to feel right and important, or else we'll tear ourselves up and be of use to no one. The point is, you can't be a good mother or good at your job when you feel guilt about those things that guilt won't change.

For working moms, celebrate the technology that can ease any longing you feel during the day. Cell phones and Skype are wonderful lunchtime or after-school check-ins for moms and kids. Some moms I know make it a practice to eat lunch with their kids every day—she from her desk, and they from the family kitchen. And when you are at home, put down the smartphone, put away your work, and be at home. Guilt may very well be a land without boundaries, but you can create realistic means of living within those boundaries that may make it more tolerable. Remind yourself: "The kids are all right" (really)—and so are you.

67

LAUNDRY IS A FAMILY ACTIVITY

✽ There are many household responsibilities for moms, but let's face it: When you ask them what their least favorite activity is, you usually hear the word "laundry"! Running the wash cycle is easy; it's the folding and the getting-it-back-into-the-drawers part of the job that seems endless. You could use a little help—and that's where, generally, coopera- tion ends.

Laundry is a function of life, and we can all participate. In fact, it can also be a learning experience and a piece of the fabric of family. It can even serve as a favor paid forward, because if you have a son, one of the best things you can do for his future partner is prepare him to do his own laundry. That is because, as anyone will tell you, a man whose mother does his laundry is a man who expects his wife to.

I was always impressed with the fact that Richard never expected me to do his laundry, and I was grateful to his mother for teaching him that task wasn't just my job. Now, there were times I didn't want him to do mine, as he wasn't very proficient with delicates, but it was sure nice to have his help. We undertook the responsibility of getting the laundry done together, although we weren't very good at delegating parts of the work to our kids. Looking back, I realize how much easier it would have been if all of us could have just done our part to take care of ourselves. In most families, the burden of getting the laundry done falls to Mom. She is overwhelmed and outnumbered as the laundry, quite literally, piles up.

Why not make it a practice to share the burden of laundry in your home? The best system I have heard of is the one where laundry becomes a family affair. It teaches each household member self-reliance and shows them that if we all do a little, a lot gets done much faster. Set up a regular Sunday schedule where everyone in the house gets a basket of clean clothes to fold and put away. Be sure the kids know in advance what time of the day is reserved for laundry, and make the tasks and workload age-appropriate (the little ones love to match socks). It's as simple as teaching your kids one rule: First things first. You want to enjoy dessert tonight? You have to eat your veggies. You want to go to the zoo on Sunday? Get those laundered clothes put away. Routines are like elixir to children, and empty laundry baskets in the hall put a smile on a mom's face! There is something about that empty basket and clean and tidy closets that make life feel more manageable. And that makes all the difference, come Monday morning.

68

WHEN TOUGH LOVE COUNTS
ON YOU TO BE FIERCE

The "Jekyll and Hyde" stories parents describe when their teens hit puberty are endless. The happiest child can suddenly move into a dark depression, or the child who has always had everything going for her suddenly begins failing in school. These are frightening times, fed by hormonal changes and the pull of youth culture. Although not every child will experience a truly serious problem, you need to be vigilant for signs that your son or daughter is going through some emotional, and potentially self-destructive, shift. When your child's behavior indicates to you that something is not right, you must be prepared to act and call on what I think of as "fierce love" to rein your child in.

Many of us have heard about the concept of "tough love," which in my mind is about the "no excuses" application of consequences for unacceptable behavior. It puts the burden of responsibility to change upon the child. "Fierce love" is something different. It is that overwhelming, undeniable maternal resolve to step in and take whatever actions are necessary to save your child. "Fierce" does *not* mean using anger or coercion.

It is instinctual; it is the life force that ties you to your child's well-being as surely as the umbilical that once connected you. It is the force behind a mother's claim, "I'd do anything for my child," or "I'd lay in that bed myself if only I could spare her." If you watch animals in nature, the mother mare will nip at her colt to correct him and set boundaries, and a whale will attack a white shark to defend her calf. There's no question about who's in charge and who's the mama. Each of us must find the strength within to know the difference between coddling and hoping a situation gets better on its own, and being grounded in the kind of love that compels you to do what you have to do when your child's life is on the line.

I've seen what it means when parents don't step it up in the area of discipline, and then a problem spirals out of control. Sometimes, really loving your kids looks like tough stuff, and sometimes, it is. Tough love often works. But there are times when our kids stand at a crossroad—times when their behavior puts them at risk. We're talking about something that is far beyond grounding them or taking away their computer time: drug abuse, blatant dishonesty, cutting class, cutting themselves, and other life-changing choices that they should not make on their own. In these situations, you are the only one who can give or get them the help they need before it's too late; you are the one to intervene and help them change their course.

It's really challenging when a good kid gets in with the wrong crowd and starts making bad choices. That's what happened to a girlfriend of mine who lost her husband in a car accident. Their son Alex was sixteen when his father was killed. Alex had always been charismatic—a good athlete and an excellent student. He was the kind of boy you hoped your daughter would marry one day. But after his dad died, he began hanging out with a different crowd. His new friends were much faster, and into some risky behavior. Before long, Alex's grades were slipping; he was late to school, and some days, he didn't go at all. Then one afternoon my friend received a phone call: Alex had been arrested for shoplifting. It all happened so fast. Even in her grief, my friend accessed fierce love. She knew Alex needed some strong leadership and guidance at this pivotal time in his life. Thankfully, the charge was dropped and my friend found an Outward Bound program for teens that would have Alex gone for most of the summer. He would miss football and baseball, but he would be removed long enough from his peers to learn some valuable lessons, guided by nature.

Honestly, one never knows what pivotal choices we can make that could alter the destiny of our kids. There are times when love isn't all warm fuzzies. Fierce love requires a deep resolve to change the motivation and environment influencing your child, and sometimes that means, as in Alex's case, securing professional help for your child, in spite of the expense. It is the kind of mentality that says you'd sacrifice yourself if you had to and throw yourself under a moving train to push your kid out of the way. If you find yourself unable to hold your kids accountable and can't do what needs to be done, it's your job to find the help you need—that's fierce, too. It's difficult to admit to yourself that you can't do it on your own, but the truth is we all need help sometimes.

We know that our teens will not make our lives easy, nor their own, for that matter. And we know that not all problems teens have are so dramatic. They will, after all, experiment just as you did when you were that age. Nor is there one fix-all solution to the big changes that happen during adolescence. Every situation is different. The point is, when the warning signs are there, there will be a better outcome when you step in early and create a plan of action. Remember that life is a process, not a destination. Call on fierce love when you need to; it will help you to help your child navigate the murky waters of growing up.

· 69 ·

FEELING SEXY FROM THE INSIDE OUT

The truly confident and empowered mom shines from within. I am often startled when people have commented to me that I have gotten "hotter" as I have aged. I'm not sure about the hotter part, but I know all that has really happened is that I have become more of who I am authentically, and am not living in my roles or in some idea of who I think I am. I haven't changed all that much; I'm still devoted to family, but I'm not confined by that role. I don't live within the narrow expectations of what some think mothers (or grandmothers, for that matter) should be—sexless and self-sacrificing—but rather have found a sense of liberation and freedom that comes from feeling fully expressed and alive. I am unapologetically me, and it shows from the inside out.

Cultivating your inner glow of confidence from the inside out comes from accessing your health, well-being, and vitality. Much of this has to do with attitude, and much is from taking chances. And sometimes it's about seizing a new opportunity, or choosing to have more fun in your life.

A couple of years ago, I was invited to take a pole-dancing class with a group of suburban moms. Half of our group was single while the rest were married or in committed relationships. None of us had ever tried pole dancing before, and we all giggled a bit nervously, given the public perception. However, it was one of the most fun and empowering classes I've ever taken—not to mention strenuous. Truth is, there is something of an exotic dancer inside all of us, and it is incredibly liberating to let her out! The studio lights were turned down low and there weren't any mirrors in the room. The instructors (both of them mothers) told us the eight of us were to share two poles. Then we got started. This class was all about getting your sexy on and feeling it from the inside out. But it was also about a form of fitness training that uses climbs and spins to increase upper body strength, and strengthen the core, and to enhance flexibility. By the time we were done, my abs had never felt so worked out. I also truly understood the value of a woman's hips. I would recommend that all married women take this class, because it helps to access sexuality in a completely holistic way.

If pole dancing seems a little extreme for you, then consider trying another form of dance such as belly, salsa, or hula as a way to express your inner goddess of love. If classes aren't your thing, then dance in the privacy of your own home to Shania Twain's "Man! I Feel Like a Woman" when no one is watching! Letting loose is the goal, and allowing yourself to be unencumbered, for a time, by your role as a mom.

Being a mom should never mean losing touch with being a woman.

No matter what your age or romantic status, celebrate your inner sense of sexuality. You will radiate with the flame of your femininity and with a light that is burning with self-love that comes through expression and self-confidence. Move those hips! Get your groove on and let your goddess shine!

70

IS THIS A SITUATION I CAN TRUST?

✿ Making that turn into middle school is a truly big transition for kids. They are exposed to much more, their world moves faster, and they definitely don't stay innocent for long. Most important, your sphere of influence competes with that of their peers, and there are pressures on them everywhere. Whether we like it or not, the world that our children inhabit is saturated with references to drugs, sex, violence, and all kinds of teenage drama. Their Disney-tinted childhoods are suddenly bold, and sometimes brazenly off-color. Things that make us cringe become "normal" to them as they move into high school. And while they are living larger and in many ways admirably more global lives than we did, they don't have to venture beyond their Facebook pages and personal computers to find ways to get into trouble. It's safe to say that it's never been more difficult or more important to do your due diligence as a parent.

Sometimes the dangers are close by, so it's important not only to know your children's friends, but also their parents, as well as other community members they encounter—their coaches, teachers, parents they babysit for, clergy, and storekeepers. You can't assume that other parents share your values, so it's up to you to check things out and learn about the families your kids spend time around. When your children come to you with a request about a playdate or sleepover, you have to feel comfortable. Ask yourself: Is this a situation I can trust?

Jasmine and Kenna attended a very protected elementary school where the families all knew each other and were loving and attentive parents that we could trust. Our elementary school was one of five that fed into one very large middle school. It seemed overwhelming to us, coming as we had from such a nurturing and intimate environment. But we also knew that it was time for Jazz to become part of a larger community, just as she would one day need to find her place in the real world. As involved parents, we felt that we could maintain control over whatever situation might arise. The first month of school, I couldn't believe some of the things that she told me regarding the rough ways of certain peers. She was offered pills and weed to purchase by some of her classmates. Some of them were already sexually active. I was shocked but also saddened that in meaningful ways Jazz's childhood seemed to be over. It reminded me of what she asked me after leaving kindergarten and entering her first-grade classroom: "Mommy, where are all the toys?" I cried at both of these transitions, realizing those tender days were over.

As time passed and Jazz's group of elementary school friends expanded to include other girls in her class, I realized that she was no longer protected by the safety net of our immediate community of parents, so I made a concerted effort to get to know the other moms. I networked to build relationships with them, I communicated openly about my values, and listened carefully and asked questions to learn about theirs. Through our conversations, I would ask about the number and ages of other siblings in the home; I asked about the relationship between the parents and how they spent time together as a family; if the mom was single, I asked if she had a boyfriend. Our conversations were never interrogations; they were always friendly and framed casually and as a way to get to know each other a little better, since our girls had become friends. But I also realized that not all of us shared the same values. For example, once I was speaking with a mother who mentioned to me the fact that her husband enjoyed hunting expeditions on the weekends. As Jazz often spent afternoons after school in their home, I took this opportunity to be reassured that the weapons were locked up and stored away.

I also found that some parents valued being seen as "cool" more highly than appearing judicious. So when Jazz would say she was going to a party at someone's house, I always called the parents to verify that an adult would be present. Once, however, I didn't ask what I would have thought to have been an unnecessary question. Jazz was invited to a sleepover. I called to ask about supervision, but it never occurred to me to ask whether boys would be invited to sleep over as well (they were). The mom I spoke with withheld that bit of information, and Jazz also conveniently neglected to tell me. After that incident, I learned to be very specific in my questions.

If you feel uncomfortable with a situation; if you don't like the answers you are getting or don't feel that the parents in charge are in alignment with your values or parenting style; or if you feel your kids will be placed in a bad situation that may jeopardize their values and safety, be ready to say "No" to them. Trust your intuition. There were occasions when I had to say "No, you can't go there." My daughters didn't like it, but they understood my intention. I never made it about them. Instead, I said, "I'm sorry, I trust you, but I won't put you in harm's way; I don't trust this situation."

71

TALKING TO YOUR KIDS ABOUT SEX

✿ This is the conversation many parents dread. Talking about sex can be uncomfortable, depending on your personal feelings around your own sexuality. Truth is, we don't like to picture our kids having sex any more than they want to think about us that way. However, we need to acknowledge that our sexual being is an inherent aspect of who we are. And, as much as we'd like to keep our kids innocent forever, they are bombarded by sexual messages; their peers are preoccupied by it; and, like it not, they are thinking about it . . . a lot. Given the combination of social realities plus their own hormonal drives, it's important for you to shape the discussion. Your voice will actually matter, and your thinking and wisdom will balance whatever your kids learn from their peers, the media, and the Internet—or worse, from their own experimentation.

It's easier to talk about sex when there is a foundation for it. That is, when your kids are small, you can minimize later problems by not making it a big deal to say the words "penis" and "vagina" and explaining the physical differences between the male and female body. It's also helpful to understand that a child's natural curiosity regarding their sexual organs starts early. It feels really good for them to touch themselves, and it's important that we teach them that it's perfectly okay to touch yourself in the bath, shower, or in privacy. It's easier to begin a successful dialogue later when you create an early environment that takes some of the awkwardness, embarrassment, or shame off the table.

A good time to open up the real conversation about sex is just before puberty. Today, girls are beginning their menses earlier than ever, and so for both your sons and daughters, it's good to consult their pediatricians regarding the right time to initiate a discussion. For girls, by speaking first with their physician, you may be able to anticipate when they might begin to menstruate, so that they will understand what is happening, and what to do, should they be away from home, or at school, that first time. Whether you have sons or daughters, however, your conversations may need to begin when they are as young as ten; for others it could be slightly later, but it should definitely take place when they are still preteens.

When you do begin to talk, you can speak to them about the physical changes that are about to happen and what to expect from their shifting hormones. There are many books that can help you ease into the conversation, and I would recommend finding one that you can read together. I like using books because it is easier to move, and deepen, a discussion from the impersonal to the personal. There are wonderful books that talk to teens very specifically about their questions—books just for boys, and books just for girls. It makes sense to preview them yourself, and to finish a first conversation by suggesting your child read at least some of the book on their own, explaining that you'll talk again at that point and answer any questions they have. Be sure to emphasize that their questions and concerns are natural and healthy, and that this is one of many conversations you hope to be having together about this in the years ahead.

The more open you can be with your own feelings about sexuality, the better the conversation will be. It always helps to keep the goalposts in your mind when you speak with your kids. That is, in the end, what you want for them is to become happy, fulfilled adults. Let's face it: Sex is important to our health and spiritual well-being, and that's why it's so important for our kids to feel comfortable with their bodies and to explore sexuality safely.

As the mother of daughters, I wanted to empower my girls to always know they had the right to choose their sexual partner, and to say "No" to any person at any time. I always talked about keeping sex sacred for love, and to help them understand the differences that boys experience at the same age regarding desire and self-control. I spoke with them very honestly, always. I told them that as they grew into adulthood, they might have more than one partner, but they would always, always remember the first. I spoke with them about the importance of self-respect, and safe sex.

My friends with sons also speak candidly with them. Often teenage boys feel incredible pressure "to be a man," but may be no more ready for such encounters than a girl would be at the same age. By simply talking about it, you can make it safe for him to abstain until he is emotionally ready. It is also essential to teach your son to respect a woman's wishes concerning a sexual exploration or encounter, right down to the last moment. As difficult or awkward as the conversation may be, rape is a very serious charge. "No" means "Stop." And, when the time comes, make sure he is equipped to protect himself from STDs or impregnating his partner by making sure he knows how to use a condom and has them available.

Whether you are the parent of boys or girls, your adolescents are ready for the physical act of sex long before they are ready for the emotional entanglements that ensue from the act. I believe the longer they can wait to become sexually active, the more gratification they will have long term, because they will carry fewer emotional wounds into their future relationships. For parents, the teenage years are long. Between the years of thirteen to nineteen, kids emerge from their childhood cocoons and fly. It is difficult, if not impossible, to keep them under lock and key. Very likely, they will make these decisions and choices on their own terms. The more you model respect for them in this area, the more respect they will have for themselves and their partners. Be clear about what you want for your kids and what your values are. Make sure they understand the need for protection from pregnancy and sexually transmitted diseases. Talk with them and listen to them. It's truly one of the most important conversations you will ever have with them, and hopefully it will be the first of many.

72

TALKING TO YOUR KIDS ABOUT DRUGS

✿ The devastating effect that drugs can have on young lives is well documented. It seems that kids today are either directly or indirectly encountering drugs at earlier ages than ever. Every parent will have to address the dangers with their children in their own way. We sat our own kids down and had a family meeting to discuss and educate them about drugs and their influence. We decided we didn't want to wait until they were exposed to drugs, and the dangers drugs present, by their peers. We took a proactive approach and began early (they were eight and ten at the time), because we knew that if we waited too long, they might find themselves in a situation they would not be prepared to handle.

We talked a lot about peer pressure—what it is and how it works. And we talked about how true friends don't make you feel bad when you don't do things they want you to. When peer pressure is eliminated as a driver—when your child is prepared and knows how to get out of a situation; knows that they don't need to appear "grown up" in order to feel confident; and knows that friends change as we grow older, and that fear of rejection is not worth the price of endangering our safety and self-esteem—then they are more apt to say, "No, I don't smoke cigarettes or weed" and "I don't drink alcohol or take pills." It's the kids who are not prepared who simply can't think of any reason not to try these things, and without a parent's loving guidance and straight talk they may feel that getting high means escape from the emotional roller coaster of feelings that all kids experience with the growing pains of life.

The importance of helping your children to understand the power of "No" and to feel confident standing up to the pressure of friends is immeasurable. Children find these situations to be highly stressful, and they often say "Yes" simply because they don't have the confidence, insight, skills, and script to say no. Taking the time to build this confidence and understanding can be a lifesaver. Here are some things to say to your kids about drug and alcohol abuse:

- Ask them what they know about drugs to see what they have already been exposed to, giving you a place to start. Open the door early for discussion, so that education becomes an ongoing process.
- Peer pressure is powerful. Teach your kids to think of themselves as leaders. That will help them feel confident, and make it easier for them to voice their opinions and feelings assertively. Talk about what "real" friends are, and how they support you without making you feel badly about your choices—even if they choose differently.

- Discuss and even act out scenarios in which peer pressure is likely to happen. Sleepovers, sports trips, concerts, field trips, and parties are often gateway situations in which your child will get on the "Yes" train or the "No" train. There are many ways to extricate oneself from an awkward situation. Use humor. Reverse the pressures and say, "If I don't want to smoke, you should let me be." Find a reason to leave: "I'm hungry. I'm going to get something to eat." Look for a buddy; it's easier to resist when you have a friend who feels the way you do. If you see someone being pressured, tell that person you support them.

- Use the Internet and books to show your kids pictures of what different drugs look like. Let them know that many drugs appear to look like candy.

- Describe the difference between taking prescription medicines for medicinal purposes versus taking them to get high. Prescription drug abuse is a huge problem in grades six and up. Lock yours away so kids can't get to them.

- Make the negative effects of addiction on the lives of all people an open conversation. Use movies and stories on the evening news to point out how substance abuse disrupts everything in your life, and how it has an impact not only on the life of the abuser himself but also on the lives of his family and friends.

- Set a good example for your children. Alcohol abuse may somehow be more socially acceptable, but it really is not any different from abusing cocaine. If you are drinking to numb out a bad day or as an escape from stress in your life, then you may be setting a negative example. On the other hand, drinking a glass of wine with a meal as a relaxing ritual used in moderation is responsible modeling.

- Even though the drinking age is twenty-one, your kids will be exposed to drinking alcohol much earlier than that. Teach them to hold on to their drink and never to put it down at a party unattended, so that nothing can be slipped into it that they don't know about. Keep reminding them of this as they grow older.

- Ask them if they are using. Let them know you are watching for signs that they are partying with their friends. Be alert to personality or behavioral changes, and keep your eyes open. Do a clean sweep under the bed now and then, and don't assume your kid is immune. Early detection of self-medicating by kids is key to the success of lifetime rehabilitation.

- When your teens ask you if you experimented with drugs when you were younger, be as honest as you can about what your experience was like. Point out how it may have put you at risk in many situations. I was too busy struggling with an eating disorder to do drugs. Nevertheless, I was always honest about my struggles as a teen, because it is more normal to struggle than not, and I wanted my girls to be open and honest with me. You may omit certain experiences that make partying seem like too much fun—and present to them the truth that fun can be accomplished without the influence of a mind-altering substances.

Life offers our kids more than enough challenges to handle besides having to deal with the pressure to join their peers and experiment with drinking and drugs. Let's be sure to give them the tools they need to say "No" to those things that will only make their journey more difficult. There are too many young lives that have been devastated by substance abuse. In every single one of those lives, there was an initial opportunity to say "Yes" or "No." Let's teach and empower our children to say "No"!

73

CHOOSING OPTIMAL HEALTH
AS A LIFELONG STUDY

✿ I live in Northern California, and am surrounded by extremely health-conscious friends who are all informed about the latest news on fitness and vitamin supplements. I already do many things right in my effort to stay healthy, but most important, I make health a priority and think of myself as a lifetime student, always open to receiving new information. Maintaining good health is like anything else; it takes practice, and you must stay interested in what's important to you.

A few months ago, a friend pulled out an article for me to read that listed various environmental agents that are said to feed cancer cells. This could be important information, especially for anyone with a family history of the disease. On the other hand, studies often seem to contradict one another, and it seems like everything causes cancer these days. Nevertheless, something on the list caught my attention—plastic water bottles, which when left in a hot car can break down and become toxic. It also made me wonder why I was still even drinking out of plastic bottles in the first place, knowing that it was also one of the worst things I could do for our environment.

The instinctive answer I came up with was twofold. First, I drink from plastic water bottles because it is easier and faster to grab one than to fill my stainless steel bottle when I go to work out. The second piece for me is that, deep down, I guess I don't think it will happen to me—I think that I won't get cancer because I live a healthy lifestyle. But I realized I could also be dead wrong about that—that many people who live healthily still get sick. Yet when there are simple things you can do to minimize the risks, but still don't, it's kind of like playing Russian roulette. As a mom of children who depend on you (and love you), it's just plainly irresponsible to keep doing things that you know aren't in your best health interests. If you're a smoker, you know that you should quit smoking. You know you need to exercise, and you know which foods to stay away from. You know that every day you make health choices that cumulatively will extend or shorten your life. And you know that optimal health is a long-term plan that takes daily discipline. Today, I spend the extra ten seconds that it takes to fill my steel water bottle.

I owe it to myself first, and then to the people who love me, to put the odds for good health completely in my favor—and so do you. In choosing to take a conscious, holistic approach to my lifestyle, there are basic things I do each day, like eating a healthy diet, exercising regularly, taking vitamin supplements, drinking lots of water, and getting plenty of rest. Yet, obviously, there are habits that I need to consider changing.

My new strategy is going to be to implement one new health measure each month that can boost my immune system and optimize my health. Now that I've given up drinking out of plastic water bottles, I plan to research paraben-free products and switch to natural shampoos, cosmetics, moisturizers, and toothpaste. I will also change my house-cleaning agents and buy products that don't contain extra chemicals or bleach. If I implement one new change per month, either by deleting something harmful from my diet or environment or by adding something positive, such as consuming one more serving of something raw each day, then I will feel the confidence that comes from knowing I am taking charge and choosing greater health.

I am committed to increasing my odds for optimal lifetime health, and to reading health studies, books, and publications, so I can keep my attention on what matters most to me. There's a great saying: "When you have your health, you have everything." It's my deepest desire to continue to thrive in a strong and healthy body right alongside my children and grandchildren, and I hope that my example encourages you to do the same.

74

SIT ON THE SIDELINES
AND DON'T SWEAT IT!

If you have children who play sports, you know that the practice schedules and matches can really take over a large portion of your life. As a soccer mom, I spent many hours watching games from the sidelines. Oftentimes, I loved the intensity of the play, especially between the girls, and admired them for concentrated and energetic effort. But there were times, I am not proud to admit, when I have been one of those obnoxious parents who yell and scream at the players from the sidelines, forgetting sometimes that they are only kids.

I wasn't alone. There were plenty of former "coaches" and "assistant coaches" of recreational teams among the parents. When you've been a coach before, it's hard to catch yourself and leave the coaching to the coaches. Then there are "those" parents—the ones who cross the line between being enthusiastic cheerleaders and sadistic, menacing presences. It seems crazy to me that we've come to a place where some schools have hired security guards to keep order and peace among the parents and spectators at games.

I went from being a screaming soccer mom to a "support, sit, and cheer" parent one day while watching some parents from the opposing team yelling obscenely at the referees. I saw their children playing their hearts out on the field during a tie-breaker, and I felt suddenly embarrassed for them. My very next thought was: *Oh my god, I am one of them!* I flashed back on all the times I, too, was overinvested in a game my daughter was playing, and I felt suddenly embarrassed for myself, too.

The nature of "club" or varsity-level sports is quite different from the sweet team experiences that our little ones first know from kickball and t-ball when—surprise—every game ends in a "tie." Older athletes and, by extension, their families are often required to travel long distances and to stay in hotels to attend soccer, volleyball, lacrosse, or basketball tournaments in order to participate at higher levels of competition. The team itself begins to feel like "family," and there is a delicious level of comfort and community that grows as a result of spending so much time together. And yet, sometimes our emotions and desire for our kids to win get the better of us. When we do this, we not only violate the rules of good sportsmanship, we can also actually inhibit rather than enhance their performance and growth.

There was one dad whose sideline behavior was often out of control. Every season, we knew we would be spending time with this family because his daughter was the team's very talented goalie. Goalie has to be the most stressful job of the game, as often the team's fortunes will rise or fall on a shot saved or not. One day, this father was even more critical of his daughter's performance than usual, spitting out a litany of complaints about what he regarded as her lazy attitude toward the game. We were at a tournament, and grant you, this was the third game of a day spent enduring 95 degree Sacramento heat. I could barely stand it as a spectator, and didn't think the kids should even continue playing in such conditions. Even so, he continued his ranting. Most times, I saw him as a character and didn't take his antics seriously, but this time I felt annoyed. I looked over at him, watching him shouting and throwing his arms up in disgust. Yelling dramatically at every move his daughter made on the field, as if it were his legs doing the running.

Unfortunately, his daughter didn't miss any of his rants, either; it only added more pressure and distraction, and her performance seemed to diminish with his every taunt. Finally, he was asked to leave the field. And how old was his daughter at the time? Twelve. At one point, before he was bounced from the game, I turned to him quizzically. I was feeling kind of prickly and I asked him, "So, Dan, were you an athlete in high school or something?" He never looked at me as he mumbled his reply. Shaking his head, he answered, "Hell no, I was way too cool for that. I was a rocker. I gave up track after half a season because I couldn't breathe." Rolling my eyes, I thought to myself, *That figures.*

The next time you head for the playing fields—or the band rehearsal, the dance team competition, the science fair—remember that what we really want is to bring out the best in our kids and give them the opportunity to shine. They deserve our support on the field, or wherever we take them. It's so easy to forget that it isn't you out there performing. Let's leave the coaching to the coaches. It's great to be an enthusiastic spectator, but sometimes, your quiet, controlled presence can be the best support you can show. Keeping it all in perspective on the sidelines makes for a better experience for everyone. While competition is important, it's even more important for sports to be fun.

75

ACCEPTING KIDS AS THEY ARE

One thing I know for sure is that our kids are as unique and infinite as there are shades of gray. They come in all shapes and sizes, and have unique talents, capacities, and gifts. Even their way of learning varies. Some children learn from listening, others are task-driven and visual, while others are kinesthetic movers and shakers. In this way, they are sometimes chips off the old block; but sometimes they are as different from us as they can be, and sometimes we can perceive those differences with concern. Nevertheless, it's our job as parents to accept them as they are and to help them build on their strengths, rather than try to fix their weaknesses.

My first grandson is a dynamic two-year-old. I can already see what some of his strengths are and also where he may have a weakness. He is a stereotypical boy in many ways and has lots of energy. Curious about the world but not having much "sit still" focus yet, he needs lots of playing time. Caden held his head up immediately after birth, and hasn't stopped moving and pushing forward since, exhibiting an immediate and intense energy to survive and embrace life. As a newborn, he grabbed for his pacifier and put it in his mouth, already knowing where his hands were when he should have been trying to stuff his hand in his mouth to find it. At five months old, as soon as he could sit up, he was already wiggling on his tummy across the room (meaning my daughter couldn't leave him alone for a second).

I have watched this child's abilities unfold with a combination of fascination and awe. To his mother, who loves him dearly, he is a project! New experiences like Gymboree class that combine energetic play with directed quiet time are great for him. At home, when his mom gathers him into her lap, along with his special pillow, her signal that she wants to read a story to him, Jasmine has learned to make it interactive. He must turn the page himself, and there is a lot of pointing at the pictures to keep it active and interesting so he will stay engaged. For a long time, a five-minute book was all he could manage. If my daughter had expected him to sit quietly throughout this time, it would have turned into a battle she could not win. But Jazz learned early on to accept Caden as he is and to work in small increments to fill his gaps in attention and learning. Caden can now focus his attention for thirty minutes, and it feels like a great achievement! I have no doubt there will be many more.

I believe that there can be good outcomes for all children. My girls went to school with a lovely girl named Kellie. Kellie was a hard worker, but because she was dyslexic, she struggled to keep up with the vigorous academic pace of high school. But from the time she was a little girl playing with her Easy-Bake Oven, Kellie just loved to cook! So her parents took every opportunity they could to nurture that interest throughout Kellie's childhood—from cooking classes for kids and teens, to sitting down with her to watch cooking shows, to hiring her to "cater" their dinner parties, to helping her get a summer job assisting the pastry chef of a local restaurant. No surprise: After high school, Kellie elected not to attend college but instead got a job in a Whole Foods bakery until she could write a business plan and open her own operation. Today, Kellie owns a successful bakery specializing in vegan party cakes and couldn't be happier.

Similarly, my friend Ariana set out thinking that it was her responsibility to pull her bookish son James out of his room to join the rest of the family for weekend skiing. They are an unusually athletic family who live in a mountain town that offers incredible opportunities for outdoor adventures. But James, the middle son, preferred to spend his time reading and listening to music, eventually teaching himself how to read and write music and to play several instruments. So Ariana gave James his space, while encouraging him gently to be with the rest of the family in their outdoor play when she could. Now, as an adult, James just graduated from a prestigious university with a degree in music composition and he has come to love the outdoors. Unlike his parents and brothers, though, his love of the outdoors doesn't come out in sports and athleticism, but rather is revealed in his appreciation of nature, which is a source of creativity and inspiration for his work. He's not a skier, but he treks through the snow. He does not ride a mountain bike, but he is an avid hiker. Above all, James is happy and has a bright future. Ariana allowed

James to be the child he was, and eventually, he became the young man who found his own way.

Often, our kids may resist our efforts to encourage our way of life—attending church services, or settling down, for instance, like we did—but as adults they may come around in their own time, and our example matters.

Sometimes what might look like a weakness when our kids are young and don't fit the mold may turn into the driving force that reveals their greatest gifts. As I think about my little Caden and his intense awareness of the world around him, I have no doubt that his assertiveness, speed, and energy will equip him well later on when he enters the world of adults and tomorrow's even faster-paced workplace.

As moms, we have to resist our urge to "fix" our children. If you are overly focused on the problem—Caden's short attention span—you miss your child's strengths—Caden can focus his attention when he is engaged, and his enthusiasm to take in his world is boundless. I urge you to see both sides of what could be a weakness in your child. Reframe the issue. This way of parenting is not only a reflection of your unconditional love, but also will enable you to do all that you can as a mom to tip the scale in your child's favor.

76

MAKE PEACE WITH THE FACT THAT
THIS IS THE BEST YOU CAN DO

A girlfriend and I were speaking the other day about how complicated midlife can be when you still have kids at home, and you also find yourself becoming the caretaker of your own parents.

My friend Lyla is the mother of five children, two of whom are still at home. Meanwhile, her mother suffers from dementia and now lives in an assisted living facility that Lyla and her husband supplement financially. They also are responsible for taking care of her emotionally, visiting her whenever they can, being sure her clothes are in order, her bills are paid, and doing light shopping for her. I asked Lyla how she managed to balance taking care of her little ones with also tending to her mother's needs, and how she felt about all this responsibility.

She took a deep breath and sighed on the exhale. She said, "Sometimes, I just feel so guilty that my mom can't live with us and has to lie in that bed waiting to die." We talked a little more and she shared the frustrations and feelings of her situation. We decided that her best strategy was to simply make peace with the fact that she is doing her best.

That on any given day, all she can do is the best she can to balance her many conflicting responsibilities. Feeling guilty when she knows she has tried her best is something she just had to let go of.

Recognizing that we are doing our best, as partners, mothers, and daughters, is something that we could all benefit from in our lives. When you are feeling guilty, it's important to notice the thoughts behind the feeling. Chances are you are living with some stale social ideals that no longer reflect the shape and challenges of our modern lives, or the reality of your situation. When we check in with ourselves and consider our situation in this way, we can free ourselves from the shadow of undeserved guilt and from the shackles of that stress.

The life of a mom is full of responsibility. We can often feel like Atlas, carrying the world as it rests on our shoulders. Raising a family while taking care of our parents and seeing them through a difficult passage in their later years can easily become overwhelming. All we can ever do is our best. We can try to plan, to prioritize, and to act responsibly, while taking solace in the fact that we are operating out of good intentions. That is the best we can do, and it has to be enough for now.

77

EMOTIONAL INTELLIGENCE
IS IMPORTANT

As mothers, we want many good things for our children. We want them to be happy, to achieve their dreams, and to be emotionally and physically healthy. We hope their lives will be free of addiction and abuse. We hope they will find a loving mate and have a sound relationship. Whatever they choose to do, we want them to be happy and successful.

Our culture has long identified achievement and success with strict measurements of academic intellect—IQs, test scores, and grades—but that has changed. This is in large part thanks to the work of Daniel Goleman, who has shown us in his book *Emotional Intelligence* that traits like self-motivation, initiative, optimism, empathy, and social competence in interpersonal relationships are key to raising the happiness quotient of our lives. It is not enough to achieve academic goals and accolades; these things by themselves do not breed happiness, great relationships, or even professional success. What matters perhaps even more is how we manage our feelings, interact with each other, build friendships, problem-solve, and manage our conflicts. Happiness and success, more than we've ever understood, are linked to intuition and intangibles like having an empathic awareness of the surrounding world and an ability to communicate and express feelings.

The most grounded, contented adults I know are those who embody these traits. Happily, we've learned to value self-expression and to encourage our kids to talk about and express their feelings. For a long while, boys and girls were trapped in stereotypes that emphasized girls' soft, vulnerable natures and boys' rational and pragmatic sides. Boys didn't cry or display emotional sensitivity: "Be a man," our parents told our brothers, while girls were considered too volatile to make it in a man's world. Today, however, we live in a political world where Hillary Clinton can become tearful while on her presidential campaign trail, and where House Speaker John Boehner can cry, too. It's okay to express feelings. Political leaders and outstanding performers in all walks of life are no longer defined just by their IQs, and a great student is not defined merely by her ability to take a test

In an earlier chapter, we talked about understanding our children's strengths and learning styles. What this new thinking reminds us is that those kids with high emotional intelligence may not be the great test-takers, but they can become exceptional human beings. They tend to be more intuitive, empathic, and creative while they navigate their world through their feelings. Make no mistake: The world needs intellectuals;

we need scientists and engineers and men and women with hard-wired IQs. But we also need to value this new paradigm that reminds us there are many varieties of intelligence. And we need to value what we can learn when we think with our hearts and feelings, and live more fully in those open spaces.

78

BREATHE AND GET YOUR
GOLDEN PAUSE

It should be so simple, but it's amazing how many of us forget to breathe. Yet, in order for you to access clear thinking and relieve anxiety and tension, your brain needs oxygen like a plant needs water. Many spiritualists believe that our breath is our path to consciousness. It is the foundation of meditation and yoga, and it brings us into the moment, where we can be completely aware and present.

Our breath is the easiest way I know to get back to our core, or to what I call "vertical." Vertical is the up-and-down line of energy, where presence resides, in the center of our being. To the left of vertical, you may be distracted by past events; to the right, you may be consumed with fear and worry, thinking too much about the future. But when you find your center core, it is easier to access your feelings from that grounded position. It is here where love and kindness reside, and from here that we want to speak to our family members, with a calm and authoritative demeanor.

We all know that stress is an undeniable part of life, and how easy it is to let all the small stuff irritate us until it builds up and we are ready to implode. With kids and the inexhaustible energy they demand, it's easy for your patience to fray. When the children go at each other the way siblings do; when they ignore your repeated requests for their attention and cooperation; when it's 5 p.m. and your head is pounding, and dinner, baths, and bedtime are still ahead; or when your teens give you attitude, it's easy to snap.

In the busyness of my life, I can veer off course and become frazzled. In fact, I can get so muddled that I begin reacting to a situation from fear, or from anger, instead of remembering to access my vertical center, from which I can respond more gently. So if I am upset, angry, tired, or about to say something I may regret later, I make it a personal practice to breathe. This is a quick strategy that really helps you to hit your internal reset button, so that you may access your mental clarity and respond appropriately.

In another chapter in this book, I introduced this same breathwork exercise, because breath and inner peace go hand-in-hand and can be applied in many different situations. Breathing before you speak helps set you up for composed communication, whereas breathing to get your Golden Pause helps you find stillness within throughout your day. Here, again, is the technique I use: Place your tongue on the roof of your mouth and hold it there on the inhale. Breathe in very slowly while expanding your belly out as you breathe in, and then shift your tongue to just behind your lower teeth, opening your mouth slightly, and hold it there on the exhale while you let the air make a hissing sound as you release it. Inhale deeply and exhale even longer, allowing sound to escape, if it's there, because this will relieve tension. Do this three times, and then pause for a few seconds, holding your breath. This will reset you and help you regain composure.

This strategy to hit your reset button and get the Golden Pause you need should take the edge off your emotions, so you can respond to any given situation with calm resolve. You can also practice this as part of your early morning ritual, to find your peaceful sanctuary and center. If you do so, you will have greater access to your wisdom that comes through being in the moment.

79

HOLD BACK AND DON'T
GIVE THEM TOO MUCH

When Richard and I were new parents, we were surrounded by friends who were also having babies and beginning family life. The first child, as you've discovered, is such a shock in so many ways. I remember wondering if I would really know how to raise a child, and how I would know everything I needed to know. Most of it you just do naturally, but much of parenting should not be done unconsciously, because it's the small things we do that set precedents that shape our kids' lives. As much as we want to give them the smoothest ride through childhood and into adulthood that we can, doing too much for our children will often incapacitate them in ways that have significant and lasting impacts on them. It really pays to hold back, sometimes, and not give your kids too much.

America is a nation of immigrants, and each successive wave has made its place here by hard work. Each generation strove to make a better life for their families. They valued education for their kids and they gave them stability, with strong cultural values and the ties of community and family. It seemed natural for that second generation to grow up to achieve a higher standard of living than their parents could, and to build a family name with more economic stability. But many families found that with that comfort came the expectations of an entitled generation. Some children have lacked the work ethic of their forebears. With the ease of each generation, the hunger to achieve sometimes loses its allure.

I was a new mom again myself not long after Kenna, my second child, was born, when I visited a friend who was on maternity leave after having her first baby. She had just changed the baby's diaper when she pulled the blow-dryer out and began blowing her newborn's bottom dry. I was stunned and asked her what on earth was she doing. Lori replied quite matter-of-factly, "Oh, I do this every time I change her, because it keeps her from feeling cold." She said this as if every parent should blow-dry their child's bottom when changing diapers. I'm not sure I did a very good job hiding my amusement at this example of "doing too much." With two girls under the age of two and a half at home, I guarantee you, I was past this kind of perfectionism. But I was also already aware of the ramifications of what can happen when you make things too easy for your children. I had made some errors in this direction myself, and would continue to. But I also realized that, at times, there was real value in the practice of a little bit of benign neglect. It really is okay to let young children cry. That's what babies do; they cry. It can even be healthy.

A woman I know and her husband picked up their three children and moved to Europe. They had become increasingly unhappy with the environment their children were growing up in—and becoming attached to—the one that allows kids to be raised with every material thing they wanted and every desire fulfilled. To be honest, they didn't much like the young people their kids were becoming.

We don't have to transplant our lives in order to withhold and in order to give. But we do, in ways that are appropriate to our circumstances and within our values, have to ask ourselves the question: How much is too much? And, will we destroy our kids' personal motivation if they have it too easy? In giving them what they want, are we taking away their understanding of how to earn it and achieve it for themselves?

The same parents who have the desire for all the right and good reasons to make life too easy for their kids when they are young shake their heads in bewilderment later, not understanding why their teens or young adults lack a sense of passion for achievement. When we do too much early on, we don't allow our children to develop their internal drive, or to feel the satisfaction that comes from wanting to make life better for themselves. Some struggle is good, and a child who learns to work hard to be successful is far better off than one who has a natural talent, but no work ethic or drive at all. Encouraging our kids to earn their privilege—whether athletics, schoolwork, or odd jobs for extra income—through hard work is one of the greatest gifts we can give them.

It's important to remember that the small things we do to show love are good, but it is equally important to question the real messages we are sending in the process of living. Resist the urge to "over-do" for your kids just because you can. Not making them too comfortable will pay great dividends later (even the Obama girls make their own beds and have chores to do). One day, you and your kids can rejoice as they take steps to achieve their dreams by working at them and they learn to live life knowing they can take care of themselves.

80

BE THE EXAMPLE YOU WISH TO SEE

This strategy playfully references one that parents of Baby Boomers used to say: Do as I say and not as I do. Truth is, kids don't operate that way. Up until about age ten, you and your partner (and any other primary caretakers in the household) are your children's greatest influence. They are watching and listening to every move you make. In fact, kids don't miss a beat, and that's why you want to be the example you wish to see in them.

I really admire how my Iranian friends have raised their children. At times, they may have looked a bit neurotic to some of us, because they were so structured in their approach. But they have done a remarkable job with their boys, who are respectful, articulate, and delightful. Clearly, they have thrived. I asked their mom how she has managed to do this, and she said she knew she had to set the example for them of how adult people behave. She said, "You can't use profanity and then chastise your children for using bad language. You must be clear about your personal values and then live them with your actions." If you want your children to value honesty, integrity, and hard work, for instance, you must embody that. If you want them to become readers, they must see you enjoying books as well. It's true our kids will do as we do.

Is there such a thing as moderation? For instance, what about cigarettes and alcohol (never mind that they are prohibited for underage children). Once again, the same rules apply. If you don't want your kids to smoke, then you should not, either. If you do drink, be sure to do so in moderation, and be sure your teens see that. Understand that teens don't like hypocrisy, but also be aware they don't yet have the rational restraints adults do. If they make a bad choice and go astray, and most teenagers will, you will be able to discipline them more effectively and hold them accountable only if they know that your values and those you are trying to instill in them are reflected by the way you live.

You must determine what kind of picture you wish to portray, and then the canvas paints itself with your day-to-day interactions and lifestyle choices. You maintain your credibility with your kids when you can say, "Do as I do," and you don't need to back it up with any other language, because you have already modeled the example for them.

81

BLENDING FAMILIES, EYES WIDE OPEN

For many women today, blended families are the new "normal." As I have watched my friends navigating this new terrain, I have to admit it's big stuff to sort out, with lots of small stuff thrown in. The agreeable novelty of a "Brady Bunch" life appeared so easy to accomplish on TV, but in reality, the joining together of a group of people, even in the name of love, requires more than a little awareness, deliberation, and patience. Blending two family units into one requires your eyes to be wide open, and should include your ex-partners, when possible.

My friend Sandra fell in love with Michael, and after they had dated for a year, she and her six-year-old daughter, Lilly, enthusiastically invited Michael and his two daughters to move into their home. They went ahead without putting any strategy in place or discussing how their life together as a fivesome might look; Sandra and Michael loved each other and they just thought things would work themselves out. Today, however, Sandra struggles with Michael's daughters' disrespect. They have made it very clear that they have no intention of helping to ease the transition, or even of trying to make it work at all. Sandra has told me that it is as if there are two separate families living under the same roof. Having no interest in becoming a "step-martyr," she is ready to move out of her own home.

Another woman I know, Holly, was on the other side of this transition and her marriage barely survived. Holly married Fred, who had joint custody of his teenage son and daughter. The kids evenly divided their time between their mother, and Holly and Fred. Today, Holly and Fred are raising three children of their own, while Fred's older kids are not welcome in their home. Ten years later, they are still attempting a successful family blend.

After speaking with my friends about the types of situations and scenarios they've experienced, here are a few Don't Sweat strategies that could help two units to blend into one:

- As two parents who are now a couple, you must make it clear to all your children that you are a united front. Your support of one another must be 100 percent. As a team, you are co-leading the blended family. Make it clear by your actions of support that you have each other's back in all situations. If the families are going to blend, you need to stand together first. You can't act as separate units any longer, because now you share the same home.

- There are issues of respect to deal with in blending families. You naturally want your partner's kids to "like" you; but the truth is, respect comes first. If there is a honeymoon period, it will be over quickly when you move in together. Respect is something you have to earn, even from children. Your boundaries must be very clear, and so must your expectations. You'll know if you have their respect or not by how they respond when you ask them to do something. For example, if you ask your partner's children to pick up their clothes or turn down their music, and they disregard or talk back to you in a manner that is sassy, then you need to sit down with them, look them straight in the eye, and remind them who is in charge. You need to stay calm but firm. Their home may also be your home, but you are the adult. You can be friends, but you are the authority. These small steps will gain big rewards. You also need to enroll your partner in the discussion as much as possible, but leave the discipline up to the biological parent.

- It's not your job to raise your partner's children, but you can be a support person in their lives. Leave the real parenting up to the parents, and don't try to replace your step-children's real "other." You want them to respect your boundaries, and you must respect theirs. No matter how nice you are or how many wonderful things you do for them, you will not win if you are trying too hard to be a surrogate mom. Be invested in supporting your partner, your relationship, and to the extend you can, to supporting his children.

- Do your best to create a positive relationship with your partner's kids by taking them on errands with you and having special dates. Often, when you separate children from their siblings and their environment, you can connect on a different level. Take time to learn about them and make your interest genuine. Accept them as individuals, accepting them just as you accept the differences in people outside your home or family. Don't accept rudeness, but learn to tolerate differences.

- Remember: Kids don't have the same maturity that you do; their brains are not yet fully developed. They are not adults and they feel threatened by sharing their dad with you. If you understand this ahead of time, maybe you won't take personally the truth that they would really rather things be as they were, before the divorce, and since that time, when they had their dad to themselves.

- Recognize that you will *all* have to bend, to blend. Discover shared values. Define together what kindness and respect look like. Make household chores something everyone participates in. Be sure you can speak to your partner regularly and with respect about his children and your issues—remember that they love him, and so do you. Allow your partner the same openness you'd like to receive as he approaches you with his own thoughts regarding your children.

- Try to have family meetings and remember that your children and your partner's children are also stakeholders here. The best results happen when you respect the process of family decision-making and recognize the value of an outcome you can all feel good about. If you can afford a counselor to help you, it's probably a good idea.

In today's blended families, it's important to remember that we have the ability to make a family transition as smooth and nourishing as possible. It may not be easy, but transitions seldom are. Let your awareness, respect, and foundation of love guide this delicate process. It is often unawareness and lack of preparation that cause dissatisfaction and drama. As you move to blend your families together, use this opportunity to build a solid foundation upon which your love and family can flourish.

82

IT'S NOT YOUR ESSAY TO WRITE

✿ Homework starts these days early, in kindergarten for many, and becomes a part of your child's life for the next twelve years. The habits you establish in the beginning matter, and while you want to be available to support and assist, if you do your kid's homework for them when they are younger, you will continue doing it for them in high school. Whether you are talking about a research paper or a college entrance paper, it's just not your essay to write.

During fourth grade, Jasmine's class was doing "The California Mission" project, where each student independently researched an aspect of Old California history and culture. The children were then expected to create storyboards and dioramas to present at a school-wide exhibition. When I arrived for the presentations, I soon realized that the parents of my daughter's classmates had stepped in and taken over their children's projects. The individual exhibitions were elaborate and expensive, and clearly neither inspired nor prepared by the children themselves. The student's oral reports didn't seem to be prepared by the kids, either. The vocabulary was much too sophisticated, the content too polished.

It's one thing to take on a project like building a model airplane together, but when it's a graded assignment, it becomes unfair to other children actually doing the assignment themselves to compete with adult parents instead of their peers. It also sends children a terrible message that condones cheating, not to mention the devaluing of their own efforts.

The same is true for homework. Homework is designed to supplement and support the day's classroom learning. But in the evening, when everyone is tired and patience is short, it can seem easier to just do it yourself rather than struggle to help your kids complete their tasks. But when you do, you are reinforcing the child's anxiety that he can't do it himself, that he is inadequate, and that perseverance is unimportant. If, on the other hand, you feel like the workload is unreasonable, it's always good to advocate for your child and conference with other parents and the teacher. I used to write a note telling the teacher if I felt my child was overwhelmed by an assignment. In later years, I was amazed at the lack of communication between the departments and faculty. Students do their best work when there is coordination, so that long-term assignments and big tests are spread out and don't pile up on the same days.

Resist the urge to write that essay or finish any homework assignment, for that matter. Instead, help your kids discover their thesis statement, and flow of ideas, or work through a math problem without doing it for them. Stay present in a discussion with them as they work through the task to achieve an age-appropriate result. Remember, it's not your essay to write. The grade doesn't matter as much as the internal reward that comes from true and honest self-expression and owning their work with authenticity.

83

YOU'LL KNOW WHEN YOU KNOW

✿ I am blessed to be a person to whom many people look for friendship and coaching during confusing times. Although the issues often differ, each individual is looking for help in making the right decision. Since so many of us deal with similar problems and concerns about parenting or managing the household finances, or issues around health, marriage, and relationships, I decided it would be worthwhile to share an insight that truly embodies a No Sweat attitude.

A friend of mine just called today. She is going through a divorce and is contemplating selling her house. She told me she received an unsolicited note from a stranger that read: "I'd like to buy your house. Please give me a call if you are interested." She asked me if I thought this was a sign that she should sell. Then she got ahead of herself and started to worry about whether or not this was the right time, and where should she go and what about a condo, or should she downsize to a smaller home? Would she qualify for a mortgage and what about her sons? Was this a bad time to move them, and should she wait? My response was for her to slow down and to get her bearings first. I told her, "You'll know when you know."

It's easy to get caught up in any problem, and to think that mulling it over in our heads will result in some sort of payback for us. We think that if we sit long enough with an issue, think about it, look at it from every angle, and then rethink it again, the right answer will suddenly emerge, like the Red Sea parting. It won't. In truth, the worry and fretting actually keep you from resolving the issue, and lock you into a stressful mode. Reminding yourself that "You'll know when you know" won't make problems go away, but it does take the stress out of the situation, quiets the mind, and—most important—creates the space for a solution to appear.

Rather than allow yourself to be overcome by racing thoughts and more anxiety, use visual imagery. Picture yourself cooking a meal. Certain things on your stove require immediate attention, while others need to simmer a while. When you place those concerns in the simmering pots, you are just putting your problem on the back burner to cook slowly for a while. The problem isn't likely to go anywhere; go about your life. When you feel clarity again, return to the issue at hand—I guarantee that, if it's a real problem, it will still be waiting for you. When it's cooked, you'll know it, and by allowing your inner calm to guide you, you will come to a resolution without so much angst and struggle.

Though many issues in parenting may seem like true emergencies, very few are. Unless your child is injured, ill, or has experienced a trauma, most of your problems can be solved with this technique. When you get into your mental "caught up" tape, it's always best to step back, breathe, and place your concerns on a back burner for a while. The problem will still be there as you prepare yourself to solve it. You can't change stress, but you can shift your relationship to it and come back to the calm resolve of your inner wisdom. Fear can often exaggerate an issue, but wisdom can also follow from it as you quell your worry. Trust in this process, and trust in yourself. What appears like big stuff may just be small stuff. You'll know when you know.

84

IT'S THE SMALL THINGS THAT COUNT

There is no greater joy than giving to others. You don't have to do much to be kind and loving in small ways that matter every day. Start at home with your family, and keep it going all day long. Every one of us can make gestures of kindness that have a ripple effect that travels far and wide.

When we speak to our children with kindness and respect, we teach them by our example how to speak to others. When they witness our spontaneous acts of kindness to complete strangers, they see how important it is to extend heartfelt compassion to the community around them without expectation of reward.

Kenna never forgot her friend Lena's birthday. She brought flowers and balloons to her door every year before school. Both of my girls were always the first to celebrate their friends and teammates, or take them something if they were injured or ill or in the hospital. I remember Kenna turning to me when she was eleven, with such delight and joy all over her face, and saying, "Mommy, it feels so good to do something nice for someone else."

One of the things that gets lost in the busyness of life is our ability to take a step back and just look into each other's eyes and send love. How simple it is to spend a moment acknowledging the people around us, in the supermarket, in line at the coffee shop or at the bank, and offer an open smile.

I was at the coffee shop yesterday when I turned to the lady behind me and began a conversation. I looked deep into her eyes and she lit up with complete presence and happiness. We spoke for several moments while we gave our orders and waited for our coffee, then went on our separate ways. It was a lovely exchange, brief and perhaps not especially memorable, but it certainly lightened the day for each of us.

We can all be open and available in small ways that require little effort, but which have a big impact. We can do it with a hello, a handshake, a short conversation, or by stepping out of line at the supermarket and letting someone who's in a hurry go ahead. We can do it by remembering to connect with the person behind the counter or delivering the mail or waiting on you in a department store, too.

And we do it when we say "hello" to the person serving us in a restaurant, and asking them, "How are you, what's your name?" before giving our order. These courtesies are more than automatic expressions of good manners; they allow us to embrace community and not forget that we all are here to share our kindness and our love in simple acts we practice as a way of life.

Not long ago, I offered a passenger sitting beside me on an airplane half my sandwich. A woman at a gas station approached me because she had forgotten her wallet and needed enough gas to get home; I added five dollars to her tank without a thought. A man who saw this exchange turned to me and said, "That's about the kindest thing I've ever seen."

It just feels good to be kind. Kindness is contagious, and we never know what great impact a single act of kindness can have. If you are kind to your kids and your partner, they will most likely be kind to others. Our children look at us, and it is the behavior we model that they remember and imitate. If you treat the guy at the car park or the girl taking your ticket at the movie theater as though they don't matter, the chances are your children will, too. In life, that sort of entitlement won't serve them well. By your own actions, help them understand that if you really do treat others the way you would want to be treated, then, like a spiral, your blessings will be abundant, because what goes around, comes around, again and again.

· 85 ·

HEALTHY MOM, RADIANT MOM

We can't be reminded too often how important it is to take care of ourselves. Healthy mothers understand that it is far easier to feel happy when your body is strong, and that true radiance shines from the source of your health and well-being as you are lit from within. A healthy mom is a radiant mom.

I have always thought of lifestyle as a choice. Living in my body has been a journey for me, and during my teens, I struggled at times. I did not truly understand and treat my body as a house for my spirit; this practice has only come with maturity. As women, and especially as young mothers, it is important to listen to the wisdom of our bodies and do the things that promote holistic physical health and wellness. This will allow us to be the best moms we can be, in harmony with our bodies.

I encourage you to check in with yourself and be honest about how you are feeling about your vitality. If your energy is low, try to make an assessment of how you've been treating yourself lately, taking note of your basic self-care practices. Have you been getting enough sleep? Eating properly? Getting enough exercise? Drinking enough water? It's not a good practice to push through fatigue by masking it with caffeine and denial. Annual physicals, including blood work, pap smears, mammograms, and monthly breast self exams are important to schedule even if you are feeling well.

It's so easy to take for granted that our bodies just work for us. When we are young, they just seem to recover fast, no matter how we punish them. Think for a moment of your body as your car and your way through life. If your car requires premium fuel in order to run properly, you wouldn't put regular gas into it, because doing so could cause damage to it or prevent it from giving you optimal performance. The same is true for your body. We have to give our bodies what they need for high performance. Being in tune with our bodies means eating healthy foods, eliminating toxins from our diets, and knowing when we're off and how to make adjustments to our routine to make sure that we are prioritizing our physical and mental health.

My own personal strategy includes checks and balances and a commitment to moderation. Like anyone else, I can slide at times. Over the holidays or at social gatherings, I'll find myself drinking more wine than I usually do, and eating rich food. So I'll compensate for a few days afterward. I'll eat more lightly and extend my workouts so that I bring my body back into balance. You have to find your own system but, overall, I ascribe to habits that include consistent exercise; relaxation time spent meditating or doing light yoga or stretching; and following a healthy diet that includes lean proteins, whole grains, and lots of fresh fruits and vegetables (I love protein-fruit smoothies as a meal). I also take vitamin supplements and watch how much alcohol, sugar, and carbs I consume, and I avoid processed foods. I make sure to get the rest that my body needs, but I'll occasionally indulge that craving for sweets (especially dark chocolate). Life is meant to be fun, too!

Taking care of yourself and your health is a lifetime commitment. While your kids may not act as if they see what you are doing, I promise you, they are absorbing your example. Someday you'll see that they will model much of what you've taught them by how you live your life. Choosing a healthy lifestyle takes discipline and personal study. It's the small acts of self-love that you perform every day, to take care of your body, that allow you to fully enjoy your life. Having experienced the miracle of growing two babies in my womb and feeling the most healthy I'd ever been, I want to feel just as good as I enter my fifties. I want to have the energy to play with my grandchildren, and to embrace this happy stage in my life's journey and maintain my inner radiance—no matter what my age says I am.

86

JUST SAY "I KNOW, THAT REALLY SUCKS"

✿ In an earlier chapter, I talk about being a container and holding space for your child's emotions. Certainly, there are times when all you need to do is be completely present, a kind of empty presence, without needing to say anything at all. It's also true that there are different kinds of listening we do as parents, and that our responses can be the key to building effective communication and a closer connection with our kids. In that spirit, I offer this, a particular strategy of listening and responding that requires practice. It can feel a little awkward for you to commiserate with your son or daughter using their own vernacular—it may surprise them as much as it does you the first few times you say the word "suck"—but they'll get the message faster and more precisely than if you used the most eloquent words you could come up with. And that's the goal is, isn't it? You want to connect.

There are times, too, when we have to resist our natural tendency as moms to "fix it." Sometimes we just can't. And there are times, as our children mature, when all they really want from us anyway is for us to just listen to them and allow them to vent. Instead of hearing our advice and the many solutions we see for their problem, what they would really like to hear is simply, "I know, that really sucks."

If we can step back for a moment and think of all the times we just feel like unloading our emotions, and see that's all it is, it's easier to relate to our kids when they need to, too. There are times when all they really need is a shoulder to lean on, someone to just listen to them, and to validate whatever they are feeling. While this is one of the hardest things to do, it is probably one of the most important acts of unconditional love and acceptance we can offer our children at any age—and our friends, coworkers, or life partner.

This is a strategy that doesn't ask you to commiserate in full sentences, or to allow yourself to get caught up in their negativity. It is more about allowing them to feel heard—acknowledging their hardship without offering advice. There is something so healing about being witnessed, even if it's something that's negative that has made you unhappy. You can hold space without offering any advice—unless, of course, you are asked.

The other day, Kenna was explaining her frustration to me over a grade on a paper she'd written for class. I began to give her advice about how she could handle the situation with her professor. She stopped me and said, "Geez, Mom, I know all that. I'm feeling upset, that's all. I just want you to acknowledge that sometimes it just sucks. Can you just say, 'I know, that really sucks.' Please?"

I have learned, and continue to learn, how difficult it is not to try to fix my kids, or my friends, for that matter. Most times, what fixes them is just having the space to speak their grievance and be accepted for who they are. If you're a positive person, "That really sucks" may not be easy to say, but try it anyway.

87

GET OFF THE BANDWAGON

As I look back, one of the greatest frustrations Richard and I had as parents had to do with the lack of control we felt when it came to the direction of our children's education and the pressure we felt to stay on a treadmill of success. Children's lives are packed with hours of homework serving a test-driven culture, and a menu of extracurricular activities—academics, sports, arts, community service—that feels like an endless checklist. The result is a generation of overburdened and stressed children inhabiting a world where academic cheating and burnout are tragically familiar. Our education system, unfortunately, is not truly geared toward a holistic education for our kids. It's a growing concern among mothers that our kids are overworked, in too many ways, and we have to get off the bandwagon culture of fear that is perpetuating a system that isn't really helping our kids stay healthy, mentally or physically.

One of the most frustrating things about raising our kids in this system is the inability to give them the kind of childhood that we had.

Baby Boomers had it the best, because there was a healthy balance between education, family time, and free time. We worked hard in school, but felt none of the desperate, soul-crushing pressure experienced by today's kids. We didn't feel nearly as much pressure to earn a high score on an AP test or attain a top percentile on the college boards.

When I look around at my personal friends and acquaintances, I see strongly directed, creative people who are well developed emotionally and really good problem-solvers in a variety of careers. Today, the race to be high achievers seems contrary to the very things that will enable our children to succeed as adults: creativity, problem-solving skills, internal motivation, and doing what they love. Now, we seem to be raising kids who flame out, or who feel their particular strengths and talents are unimportant and give up. Education models that devalue children and their whole education in favor of rote learning and regurgitation to test to the standards beat the passion out of our children.

Schools feel the pressure, too. Schools load on the homework because they have external measurements to meet. We experienced the crush as early as fifth grade, as Kenna was doing three to five hours of homework a night while beginning her club soccer career. We talked to her teacher constantly about how crazy the workload was, but she assured us she was only getting the kids ready for junior high. Recently, a young friend was hired to be a teacher for a charter school. She was told: If your test scores drop in your class, you will be fired.

With this kind of intense pressure on teachers to perform and teach to the standardized test, the only recourse we have as parents is to become our children's advocates. It takes courage to make change happen, and it begins in every home. You are the expert about what your kids need. You will be the one witnessing the common signs of stress: headaches, stomachaches, sleep issues, and anxiety attacks. If you sense that your child is in trouble, you need to act. Here are some ways you can advocate for your child by creating reform in your own home:

1. Speak to the school administration about creating mental health forums and seminars for parents, so they can be informed of what high stress looks like in their teen.
2. Develop a relationship with your children's teachers, so that you can communicate with them about stress issues.
3. Implement a homework cut-off policy: one half hour per subject (English, math, science, and social studies) of uninterrupted time (meaning no TV and no social media interaction). You need to be the one to tell your kids that enough is enough when they are given too much to do. Choosing balance over stress is important for the whole family.
4. Encourage your child to do his or her best to develop a deep understanding of the school material, and encourage what they enjoy about learning.
5. Prioritize family dinners.
6. Encourage after-school sports and playtime.
7. Make sure your kids take one day off per week from homework (Saturday or Sunday).

8. Allow for occasional "mental health" days at home, if your kids need a break from the stress.
9. Encourage them to talk about their feelings.
10. Discourage bragging about test performance, making successes internal and minimizing the damaging effects of failure.
11. Encourage your children's natural gifts by supplementing their education with outside enrichment.
12. If your child is overly stressed, bring it to the attention of the school counseling program and enlist the administration's help.

I encourage you to speak out! The more parents who step forward and lead the way, bringing their concerns about stress out into the open and getting off the bandwagon—rejecting the cultural fear that "if my child doesn't keep up, he won't have the opportunities other kids have"— the more likely change will follow, balance will return, and our children can enjoy both health and a love of learning.

88

THERE IS A COLLEGE FOR EVERY KID

✿ We are told how competitive it is these days to get into the college of your choice, and how this creates tremendous pressure and a deep worry about the future. The stress begins for many families very early, and here I underscore the word "families." It may be your child who is going to college, but the search and application phase has the look and shape of a team activity. Families seem so invested in the details and decision-making that one wonders, whose education is this, anyway?

When I talk to moms of college-bound kids, I often walk away with a gnawing feeling that it's all about ensuring the result, and not about the process. Sure, we want our kids to attend the best school they can— whether it is an Ivy, another private institution, a state university, or a two-year college. (In fact, for many young people, attending community college is a terrific idea that allows the student to save money while fulfilling basic requirements, before transferring into a university for a strong finish.) But when parents take over—deciding which schools they will allow their child to apply to, working on the Personal Statement (aka college essay), sometimes even editing it to such an extent that the child's voice is lost, and in casual conversation using the word "we," as in, "we" thought this about University X or "we" liked College Y, when the parent really ought to be using "he" or "she"—something is wrong.

The point is: There is more than one right college for every student. So parents have to relax. As a mom, you can let go of the pressure you feel to have your child attend the school of your dreams, and make it about encouraging him to own the process. That is, it's your child's responsibility—not yours—to do the homework: research schools, plan visits, complete paperwork, sign up for testing, request teacher recommendations, complete financial aid forms, look for scholarships, and all the other tasks. That is the essential part of applying to college. Your role is to assist, not manage. Your child may also have very different ideas from you about where she sees herself for the next four years. A parent may have an attachment to a specific institution, usually their own, or one they feel is especially prestigious. It may be all wrong for the child, but no matter. Parents push, but when they do it's usually because they believe that where their child goes to school is a direct reflection of how well they did as parents.

The truth is, your children's accomplishments, or lack thereof, are not a report card of your performance. It is not about bragging rights, but stepping back and celebrating the process as a reflection of your child's own performance in high school and everything they have learned along the way about responsibility, meeting deadlines, organizing their time, expressing themselves, and advocating for themselves. In other words, applying to college is no more than a reflection of where they are on their personal journey. College is a big step, and they will grow exponentially over the next four years. For now, before they are gone, and while we still have them, we want to empower our children to find a place for themselves that is like the shoe that feels just right. We do this by letting go, and letting them manage the details and make the final decisions. Giving them this space and support will also assist them in revealing more of what they have to contribute to the world in terms of their talents and gifts. By letting go now, before you have to, you are giving your child the gift. You are saying, "I believe in you. You're ready."

In the application process, I found it helpful to work with a counselor who helped my girls look for the colleges that were a good match for them. We were looking for the right fit. We looked at location and size, and we chose colleges that were searching for students like them in terms of their grades and interests. As your child begins his search, here is a short list of questions for him to think about as he—not you—makes his decision:

- What kind of school environment, equipment, facilities, and housing do I want?
- What kind of program do I want to pursue?
- Do I want to attend college in an urban, suburban, or rural environment?

- How far away from home do I want to be?
- What sorts of support services are available if I have academic or personal difficulties?
- What is the social life like? What sort of extracurricular activities are offered? What do students do on weekends? Do they stay on campus or leave the area? What about sororities and fraternities, and what alternatives exist to Greek life?
- Who teaches freshmen?
- Is diversity among the student population important to me?
- How do my qualifications compare with those of students accepted in the past?
- What are my strengths and weaknesses as a learner? In a social setting? What does this tell me, and how can it guide my choices?
- What do I need to be successful academically?

Don't sweat the pressure when it comes to college admissions. There really is a school that wants your child, and sees the same promise and potential in him that you do. Keep things in perspective, and chances are your child will choose the one that reflects the next step on his journey.

89

PREPARING FOR AN EMPTY NEST

❀ It's natural for our identities to become wrapped around our role as mothers. When I gave birth to Jazz twenty-two years ago, and then to Kenna two years later, the one thing that became very clear for me was my purpose in life. My career path had never completely filled that longing the way my children did. For years, what felt most right in my life was the loving relationship Richard and I shared, and the completeness of our family unit. Even though I will never say that raising a family has been easy, I know we lived in a flow of flourishing love where, for a long time, we all thrived.

Life changes, though, and so did ours. My greatest transition happened when Richard passed. Early on in my grief, I remember thinking how strange life would be when my girls were both in college and left the nest. That time in my life with Richard was supposed to be ours, a time for us to rediscover ourselves and each other, and to align our relationship again with a new focus and direction. We were very much looking forward to this not-too-distant time.

When he died, I learned how to grieve and let go of those expectations of how my life was supposed to have been. I also learned to surrender to, trust, and accept what I could not change. Letting go of my kids, when the time came, was a new loss; but this time, the process was far easier and—surprisingly—a welcome transition.

Jazz graduated from high school and went to college only eight months after Richard died. While freshly stricken with grief, we quickly shifted from a household of four to two. Three and a half years later, when Kenna's graduation approached and she prepared for college, I felt new trepidation at the pending changes coming my way and spending so much time alone. There is sometimes great anticipation that comes before big change happens, and it is part of the process of letting go.

I have discovered that we grieve change and transitions, for the things we have not yet accepted, and that many women grieve the empty nest. Your role as mother changes substantially, and the more identified you are in that role, the more dislocation and emptiness you may feel. While grief is a natural emotional response to all kinds of loss, going through the grief process can eventually help you to heal. It is important to understand its benefits as a great healer. Allow yourself to feel emotional feelings of loss, to surrender to the fact that grief will guide you through this stormy passage, and will prepare you to enter the next time period in your life with renewed passion and strength.

Last year, I was flying home from a trip, and I sat with a lovely couple whose children are the same ages as mine. Their family structure and story were very traditional and, I have to admit, I was a little envious they were still together, solid in their long marriage and looking forward to their next phase. Even so, the woman confessed to me that she was scared and unsure about where she would place all the energy that she had previously poured into her family. I nodded, knowing that she had an adventure ahead, an opportunity to inquire into and rediscover her individuality. This could be a time for her to reignite interests that had long been placed on hold while she raised her children.

If you are blessed to be in a relationship, look at the possibility of rediscovering each other when you have an empty nest. Think about the attention you can finally give to each other and the things you want to do together with your new liberty. Like crazy kids again, you can make love in the afternoon with the bedroom door open and walk around your house naked if you choose.

After I got Kenna moved into her dorm, I adjusted to the still house and the "new normal" more easily than I thought I would. Having already been through so much change, I found that I actually really enjoyed having my own space for the first time in my adult life.

Life prepares us to be ready for our kids to fly, and yes, there are days when I miss the chaos of school routines, the chatter in the house, and the sleepovers with friends, the full refrigerator—and the full calendar. But I have been honest with myself about a few things.

Rather than see the empty nest as a door closing on a wonderful time in my life, I choose to see it as an opening that allows more time for me, the emptiness as a container waiting to be filled with something new and just as wonderful. It is ironic and perhaps no coincidence that our children leave at the time in our lives when we are most confident, wise, and even healthy. It is our most powerful time as women, and it is nothing to be afraid of. I surrender to and trust in this next chapter of my story, and know that no matter how far my birds may fly, they also may return home again. My nest may not be completely empty for long.

If you are just starting out on your path as a parent, it's hard to imagine that there will be a time when your little ones are ready to leave the nest. It will happen. The years pass swiftly, and the time for rediscovery and reinvention will come. As I step into this encore phase of my life, I say, Bring it!

90

HEALING YOUR BODY IMAGE,
LOVING YOUR CURVES

✿ Even though we're moms, we still peer into the mirror, searching for the lithe young body we once had before giving birth. That image still stalks us, but as mothers now, it's time to heal that. Giving our families a solid foundation of self-confidence and true self-esteem can only grow from our feminine seedling of self-love. Self-love is the greatest gift we can give our families. It starts with letting go of the old patterns and beliefs about our appearance that go back to our teens. Unfortunately, not a lot has changed since that time. Media images presented in our culture need to celebrate the femininity of our bodies just as they are, while we ourselves must stop trying to emulate airbrushed versions of Barbie dolls that are neither attainable nor sustainable images we can aspire to. And we need to seriously think about what sort of body stereotypes we are promoting for our children.

As a mother of two daughters, I am especially sensitive to this issue. I spent years of my late teens and early twenties recovering from an eating disorder. I realized when I was pregnant with Jasmine that I didn't want to pass down the body image issues that I had struggled with for so many years. I didn't want to project on to her the media image of Victoria's Secret perfection that had complicated my idea of what my body should look like. Truth is, in this world of digitized photography, photos are routinely enhanced, bodies reshaped by a computer, and hair and makeup professionally styled. The image we aspire to is not even real; it's been altered and retouched.

Over the years, I had healed the binge-and-purge cycle of my youth, but I still had to own and accept my body. Bearing children is a game-changer. I learned to celebrate my new feminine curves—the wider hips and the breasts that hung a little lower—which signaled I was no longer a girl but a full-fledged woman. I found, to my surprised delight, that I felt more beautiful than I ever had. With my daughters always watching me as their primary example, I made an effort never to talk about my weight around them. If I indulged in any complaint, it was with a close friend in confidence. And, I gave up dieting for good.

Today, I think of "diet" as what I eat to maintain health and vital, life-sustaining energy. And I really enjoy good food, too; a healthy appetite is a strong sign of physical well-being and vitality. I exercise not because I am trying to lose weight, but because I want to have physical strength and because it just feels really good. I also got off my scale and decided that I would rarely weigh myself, so that strength and fitness would be my focus, rather than a number. I take care of my appearance, not to look younger than I am, but to feel the best that I can for the age that I am. I'm happy to say that both my daughters are beautiful, and neither one of them has struggled with the body image issues I did in my youth. This is a real success story for me; I'm proud that this is something I did not pass down to the next generation.

A good exercise that I now practice is to stand in front of the mirror and send love to my body. I embrace those less-than-perfect parts of me, and have even learned to look at my cellulite and send love there, too. Learning to embrace my body the way it is has allowed my self-love to grow, and my confidence as a woman to shine.

We can wear our shape with joy, knowing that we gave birth to a new body, and embrace life after children. I know that celebrating my figure as it is and living moderately and with healthful mindfulness is better than harsh rules and regulation. I have learned that there is nothing more beautiful than a woman who recognizes her own beauty. I celebrate my femininity and my well-earned curves as I say to myself, "I'm not fat, I'm feminine."

91

STEPPING OUT TO STEP BACK IN

❀ I really want to encourage you to take advantage of those times you can find in your busy schedules to get away. We all get caught up in routine. There is nothing that will suck the life force out of you faster than waking up, dreading another day of the same 'ol thing. I've been there, too, and when I am, I know it's time to shift from existing to living.

Getting away from your routine for a day or longer (if possible) will do wonders for helping to regain your healthy perspective. In life, it's never about what you do; it's always about the attitude you bring to each moment. When you're in the eye of the hurricane, it's often difficult to believe that the drama, or the exhaustion, will ever pass. Repetition— and that's what drives most of our days—can crush one's spirit. Life starts to feel like a steamroller. My friend, whose four kids are under the age of fourteen, called the other day to apologize for not getting back to me (can you believe that!). She explained, "I feel like I am doing so much all the time, it's all a blur to me. I think I need to take a step out, so I can step back in. Then I can enjoy my kids again and be present in my own life." Hence, this strategy: Step out to step back in.

When Jazz and Kenna were little, Richard and I worked it out so I could visit a friend for a weekend now and then. Lisa didn't have children yet, but I was in the grip of mommy-hood with a preschooler and toddler at home. I realized that I was exhausted by the routine, and was feeling suffocated and trapped. Getting away helped me see small ways I could take breaks, so I would feel less overwhelmed. Stepping out helped me to rejuvenate my spirit, and also to lift me out of my internal rut so that when I returned home, I would do so feeling refreshed and energized.

Getting out of your life for a little while will help you see new paths for negotiation. Giving yourself the time away so you can return feeling more happily engaged in your activities brings new perspective, and often puts the bounce back in your step. And that is a gift for the whole family.

92

SURRENDER, TRUST, AND LET GO

✿ While we may attempt to exercise control over the clutter and craziness of our lives through adhering tightly to schedules and plans, or by being overprotective mothers, sometimes the best way to achieve a sense of balance and equanimity is to just let go. Yet, as a mom, I have found myself, at times, holding on tightly. But, oftentimes, surrendering and letting go of your worries, fears, expectations, plans, and sometimes your schedule, can relieve the stress that robs you of your happiness and joy.

The best-laid plans often take on a life of their own. Being more malleable will help you solve problems and access serenity in the middle of chaos. Most things I have ever planned ended up snowballing on their own into something I hadn't expected, and have often pleasantly exceeded my expectations. The moms who carry the burden of perfectionism on their backs like pack mules always seemed pinched and unhappy to me. I have learned that life itself is perfect in its imperfection, and if I hold on too tightly, I squeeze out the magic of the moment. Practicing small acts of surrender helps prepare you to let go more as your kids grow.

As we raise our families, there are many small and great opportunities to practice surrender. I know that you can relate to the spiral of surrender and what happens to your day, for instance, when your child wakes up with the stomach flu. Like a ball of yarn unraveling from the center, all of your plans fall apart as you surrender yourself to a day of nursing and cleaning up.

Unlikely though it sounds, potty training for toddlers requires surrender, too. You may decide that right now is the right time for your little one to get out of diapers, but until they are ready, potty training can be extremely frustrating. If you are trying to control the timing and your child isn't interested, no matter how many little charts with gold stars you create and cute big-boy and -girl packets of underpants you purchase to induce your child, it won't happen. What you call "accidents" will continue far longer than if you just surrender and wait. (As someone once reminded me, no adult has ever walked down an aisle wearing diapers.)

I remember how difficult it was to surrender my worries and fears when each of my daughters drove out of the driveway by themselves for the first time. Those first two years of driving require much letting go of what you cannot control, and trust that you've taught them everything they need to know about safety on the road. I would feel secure enough with their driving on local roads, but our freeways, with their lane-changes and faster speeds, were another story. It wasn't only their driving I worried about, but also the drivers around them who may be reckless, and my imaginings made my stomach do cartweels. Whenever I felt the contraction of fear that made me want to hold on tightly, I had to force myself to let go and surrender, because control is only an illusion.

Life is a big experience, and we will have the smaller issues of letting go to prepare us for the bigger ones. There are times we are faced with circumstances and situations of such magnitude that all we can do is practice surrender to life as it presents itself. Make the best of the moment at hand. Go ahead and make your plans, but know that flexibility is your best ally.

Change what you can, but surrender to what is. Trust that all will work out somehow, some way. And accept that no matter how much you would like to control all events and outcomes, life may have a different plan. If you practice surrender and trust, you will be well on your way to receiving the peace and serenity that allow you to survive any storm, and thrive with resiliency and joy.

93

A CIRCLE OF SUPPORT
FROM GIRLFRIENDS

It can be a journey for many of us to find those special women in our lives we can trust, but when we do, they are the gems we can't live without. I know that I wouldn't be as good a mom without my girlfriends, and I wouldn't see life as such a treasure without the women in my life who have been like angels to me. I've always told my daughters that men may come and go in your lives, but your girlfriends will remain with you in crises until you can stand on your own to rebuild your life.

In another chapter, we spoke about the value of finding other like-minded moms in your life. They pull you through the early, uncertain years of motherhood, through the newness and the isolation. Some of these women will be keepers—true friends with whom you develop a deep understanding and affection over many years. You may also find that those relationships won't survive as you become more rooted in your community, work life, and in your role as a mom of growing kids. Some older moms I know retained their early friendships; others found their friendships drifting apart as new opportunities, interests, introductions, and associations widened their circle of acquaintances. You will find yourself belonging to many social circles over the years. Some may involve the men in your life, or your kids, your neighbors, church group, book group, and so on. Your closest circle will crystallize naturally, and they will become as dear to you as family itself.

My best girlfriends and I often joke that we could marry each other (metaphorically speaking). Somehow, when women connect in friendship, they become attuned to each other's needs and feelings. They know when to just listen and love, and they know when to tell us what's up when we are a little off the mark. They support us with the gentleness of a nursemaid and the wisdom of a sage. It's safe to say that our girlfriends are there for us whenever we need them, and also when we don't, but simply need to pull out of our wife/mother lives and just giggle, shop, or chat about nothing—and everything. All we have to do is allow them to give us their interest, attention, and loving care, and receive it without apology, just as we give it back to them.

It's important to do your best to take care of those special sisters on a regular basis, because all relationships need a nurturing balance of giving and receiving. Spend quality time together going on hikes, taking a class, hitting the sales, celebrating each other's birthdays, and of course, having the occasional girls' night out away from those pesky partners, spouses, and kids! The time that you spend nourishing those bonds and sharing in laughter and support, celebrating success, sharing tears of sorrow and the rage of frustration—these times that you spend together pay off in spades when the stakes are high in crises.

There are plenty of times of change and transition in a woman's life. Having support from your friends during these times is priceless. The women in my life rallied around me, like a circle of love and protection, when my marriage ended with the devastating blow of Richard's sudden death. My special girlfriends, with whom I had shared my day-to-day life in nurturing hours of conversations on long walks, or meetings for coffee, or sitting in each other's kitchens while our kids played, or the fun times at soccer games and on school committees, these women became a tribe of strength and fueled my courage to live on. They were there to see me and my family through that time of turbulence and the very difficult transition that followed. I don't think I could have made it the distance without them.

Never underestimate the power of women as we come together to help each other in times of need. The friendship between women is as essential as air. Your sisters will stand in the fire with you and hold your space, lovingly, while you rise out of the ashes of even the most difficult circumstances. It isn't just the meals they bring or the comfort of their presence and the gentleness of their voices, as they speak in hushed tones that helps; they offer love in small ways that tell you, without speaking the words directly, you are not alone in your crisis.

It's safe to say that your girlfriends will have your back when times get tough. They'll sweat the small stuff for you, while you get back on track to a better day and a new tomorrow. Love to all the sisters who support the women in their lives! There's no greater gift you can give than to see a mother through a difficult time. Then, when it's your time, the circle will come back around, and because you have given, you shall receive.

94

GRATITUDE GROWS WITH TIME

❀ It doesn't matter how much you have, at least not in the material sense. Truly appreciating your life begins with noticing the small stuff that matters most and isn't material at all. No matter where you are in your life or what your circumstances are, if you focus on the good stuff, it will facilitate your experience of life. True gratitude happens by having a sense of contentment, and a full heart, and often this comes with practice and the passage of time.

Many things about life simply become invisible to us, lost in our distracted monkey minds. Caught up in our thoughts and activities, we can miss the gentle breeze that ruffles your hair. The magic of a spring rain. The colorful symphony of the fall foliage. The cloud formations that appear like a Monet in the sky.

While I have always loved being a mother, it has proven to be a job that's never done, and that comes with many highs and many lows. No one, of course, has an attitude of gratitude every day (unless perhaps you are the Dalai Lama) and I think it's always important to allow yourself to be where you are at all times, without guilt. Gratitude isn't something you can fake. As busy people with full lives, our level of appreciation of it changes every day, just like the sky.

In fact, life looks very different when we look back, especially when raising children. Sometimes gratitude is best measured from the rearview mirror.

I wasn't always grateful in every moment, or every day, but I do have very special memories of my children that came from a true awareness and intention that I didn't want to miss this time. Small children have a way of being our best teachers in the art of appreciation. They have a way of making fun out of anything, and what can be more important than that? Kids can take a box and turn it into a house, or play music by gently tapping on glasses one by one. They sing when they wake up, and they play with imaginary friends. The best thing is when those small hands pull your face to theirs, and you look into each other's eyes with complete presence and they tell you spontaneously "I love you, Mommy."

The later years were memorable, too. Soccer tournaments and shopping for prom dresses. The sounds of teenage chatter and laughter when the girls' friends were over. Family picnics and hikes along the coastline. Beach days and sand castles. Gingerbread houses, coloring eggs, and carving pumpkins. The triumphs. The tears. Hanging out. First dates. First kisses. First babies. Lots of laughter. Hot chocolate and long talks into the night. High school graduation. You don't want to miss a moment of it—and as I think about it now, I wouldn't give back one sleepless night, not one load of laundry or chicken nugget dinner. Being needed, and needing them. It goes by in a flash. Yes, there have been sacrifices, but the truth is, I feel so blessed with the privilege of being a mom and the gifts these children have brought to my life.

As a grandmother, I relish the small things now that perhaps were not so attractive when my own kids were little: hands that leave prints on all my windows and mirrors, and Caden's sweet angel voice when he comes to my house for our regular playdates. I soak in his presence and a true feeling of thankfulness that I get to experience these precious times with him and see him grow, inch by inch.

Children have a beautiful way of helping us to see the world through new eyes, but it's not always easy to count your blessings when your hands are in dishwater, or when it's bath time or bedtime and you have many hours to go before you can call it a day. Try to do it anyway. Count your blessings, and make the time you have together count. Receive all of the goodness that is around you, because it will change, and time flies fast.

95

WHEN THEY FLY BACK HOME

Now that I've raised a family, I know I've served my kids well by doing many things for them, seeing them through the trials and tribulations of childhood and middle school, and helping them get through the academic rigors and social pressures of high school. For those of us who've been there, too, high school graduation presents us with challenges as well as opportunities. We anticipate that the empty nest may be quite difficult, but not surprisingly, we get used to it, and even thrive in our new lives. We make the changes necessary to go through the passage of letting go, and then it's summer again, or we've celebrated another graduation (those four years go fast!), and our adult children come back home. Now what? I have learned that it's best to think of this time as beginning a new relationship with your child, and also to view it as a temporary intermission in his or her journey.

My daughter's first semester at college flew by. When finals ended and she came home, she evaluated the experience and concluded that perhaps a different school would fit her better. This decision also meant that she would have to move out of the dorm and back home in the interim.

While I was happy in many ways to have my daughter home, I quickly realized that we were both ready for our independence, and that this was a setback to our newfound freedom. For the first time in my adult life, I had lived on my own and was really beginning to enjoy the space and having little more to be concerned with than taking care of myself. The empty refrigerator, the surprisingly few loads of laundry I had to do, and the always tidy house (including the girls' empty bedrooms) made the transition particularly pleasing. After twenty years of caretaking and responsibility, I saw this time as a well-earned privilege.

To preserve this sense of independence for both of us, I had to set new boundaries right away and lay down the new "landlord" law to let her know that "home" meant something quite different after you turned eighteen. "Home" was no longer a resort with room and maid service. Even now that my daughter is back in college, although living at home, I made it clear I would no longer be her personal assistant and life manager in the same ways I did when she was growing up. Now she must do things such as book her own doctor appointments, register for classes, buy her own groceries, do her own laundry and dishes, and all those other chores. She must also respect my home and my space by keeping her things organized and clean, and must ask permission to have her friends over. I don't elect to be the college "party house."

I have also made adjustments to my own expectations. I don't keep as close track of her comings and goings. She doesn't have a curfew, but

I ask her to let me know if she's going to be out all night so I can lock up the house. We text often to check in with each other, but I don't judge how she is spending her time, or with whom. Though living under the same roof, neither one of us has certain "rights" anymore. Her study habits are her business, just as they would be if she were living away in a dormitory. In short, we have adjusted to become more like housemates, but I have the respect due a landlord.

I will always be my daughters' mother, but my feelings of responsibility have shifted as I embrace this time in my life. It is "my time" that now gets a higher priority, and I am less focused on making sure everyone else has what they need. I see it as my daughters' job to take responsibility for their own lives and to manage their own physical and emotional well-being, while I stay on the sidelines cheering and supporting from a greater distance. If I've done my job right, that is all they need.

With our national economy today, many families are having to share a living space again to save money. When your children fly back home, you want to be clear that this is a time for you both to begin a new relationship that allows for the independence everyone needs, while retaining the interdependence that defines strong families. And, as we settle in with new boundaries and expectations, you will find that you are now, finally, no longer "parenting" but becoming friends with your adult children.

96

YOU ARE ENOUGH AS YOU ARE

❀ As I've been writing this book, I began to feel a tremendous sense of loss and a tinge of guilt that my girls are now grown, and that the things I didn't do cannot be done. (This random thought keeps coming up: I wish I had baked more cookies!) Then a friend who watched me raise my children, while tending to her own, said, "Oh, Kris, you were a wonderful mother. I think you've just forgotten how many things you did right during that time. You're having selective memory just now."

Unfortunately, many women look at the deficiency model when it comes to seeing what's wrong and in need of improvement in their lives, as opposed to looking for all the things that are right and good. For every mistake you've made or thing you could do better, you've likely done one hundred things right. You are no doubt a very conscientious mother, and probably a bit of a perfectionist, too. You have to tell yourself that you are enough as you are.

This is not to say we should give up on improving ourselves. Life pushes us forward, and moving ahead means, in part, trying to enhance how we live. As women, we need to show ourselves the same compassion that we show others and give ourselves a pat on the back for a job well done. We perform many roles: We are mothers, daughters, sisters, professionals, and friends. We are continuously performing tasks and rising to the many challenges each role tosses our way. It is important to remember that we are human first. Life is about so much more than scoreboards and checklists.

Most important, remember that you are the ideal mother for your children. In fact, you were mail-ordered by divine selection. Your children need you more than any other person on this earth. You are as special to them as they are to you. You belong to each other, and you have within you everything you need to care for those little people as they grow into adults.

I guarantee it won't help secure a better childhood or future for them, or you, to beat yourself up when you feel like you've blown it. There is nothing to gain by looking back and feeling inadequate. Remember to view your life with a larger scope, and see the big picture of how you provide love, affection, and nurturing care. There is no such thing as a perfect family or mother, any more than there is the perfect childhood or the Easter Bunny. The challenge is to see how life unfolds divinely, with all of the apparent imperfections a part of the process. Just be the best you can. Being the best person you can be counts more than being a static, unchanging example of perfection. Further, the small stuff that happens will not be remembered as much as the big love that we provide. Practice looking at yourself in the mirror with kindness and saying to yourself, "I am enough as I am." Realize that you can't be all things. As we learn to accept ourselves as we are, we can begin to embrace the people in our lives with the same level of compassion. When we can notice the things we do right, then we can begin to see that all of life's circumstances and people are perfect in their imperfection.

97

PRACTICE PRESENCE

The greatest gift I can offer the people in my life, as well as myself, is living from my heart, in this moment. It is by being in this moment that I can connect at the deepest level. In this precious moment, I can become a world-class listener or doer as I bring my full attention to the people I love. When I practice presence, I am most authentically me, and am the teacher, sister, parent, and friend that I want to be.

We all say we have a "best time of day." Some of us are morning people; some of us are best focused and most productive late at night. When you practice presence, however, you bring your attention and awareness away from distracting thoughts, whatever they may be, and into full alignment with the moment, wherever you are. When you clear your head of all its yesterdays and tomorrows to focus on what is right here, your best time of day is right now.

This idea of living presently seems so simple. Yet, contemporary culture, with its exploding technology and emphasis on social media, undermines that. Connection, it seems, is either filtered or divided. We congratulate ourselves for our ability to multitask, but honestly, every time we do, we pull away from something else. Many times, I have been out to dinner and I have looked over at two people sharing a meal together in a restaurant, and instead of talking to each other, they are texting other people on their phones. And when they are doing that while driving, we also know that not living presently can be deadly.

These are the obvious ways we fail one another. By not being present, we also let down our loved ones and allow the simple gifts of a day with them to slip away unnoticed. How many times has your mind been somewhere else while your children are talking to you? What mom hasn't been jolted back to the moment by her child's insistent plea, "Mom, you're not listening"? As mothers, we live instead by the tick-tock of our conditioned busyness. Instead of embracing the gift of presence, we worry about the unattended paperwork on our desks, or the meal we need to begin preparing, or getting the family organized for school holidays. We cut the memory-making moment short and promise ourselves, "Next time," while dwelling on a future that hasn't happened or events from the past that we cannot change. As moms, we think we have all the time in the world with our kids, while the reality is, all we really have is this moment.

Our children, especially the small ones, are our best teachers of what it truly means to embrace the moment, or what the spiritual teacher Ram Dass called "Be(ing) here now." Children are completely tuned in, their minds uncluttered by expectations, belief systems, and egos that create fear and distraction. They seize life with complete enthusiasm and immerse themselves in whatever captures their attention. I love to spend as much time as I can with my little grandson. I am always in awe of how captivated he is with a garden hose or with plastic kitchen bowls and a whisk. During our afternoons together, I put my cell phone away so I am completely there to drink in the joy I feel as I watch him play. I don't want to miss a moment, because now I am wise enough to know how fast time flies.

Bringing your attention to the here and now takes practice and mindfulness. It also requires you to first abandon the illusion that we can control all aspects of life. The truth is, we can control some things in our lives, while with other things we have no more control than we do over traffic lights, the tides, or the weather. So take inventory of your thoughts and exile those that distract you. When you practice presence and live mindfully in the moment, you will think more clearly, breathe more deeply, partner, parent, and friend more completely, and truly enjoy your life more fully.

Remember to live this moment and each day as if it could be your last, and you will experience greater joy and deeper fulfillment. Let yourself go, and be here now.

98

LOVING ADULT CHILDREN

In motherhood, much as in life, it seems like just when you've found all the answers, they change all the questions. My children have gone through many changes and met many challenges, some of them smaller than others. Whether it was separating from us when they started preschool, or suffering the woes of being a teenager, or dealing with the really big stuff of life, like the loss of a father or an unplanned pregnancy, the one thing I know is that for your kids, as for all of us, life is never a smooth sail. Things fall apart for our adult children just as they did when they were kids. (In fact, things still fall apart for me sometimes, even now.) During these times, your best strategy is to see yourself as a creative counselor assisting them in restoring order and putting their lives back together. Your job with adult children who have adult problems—whether with jobs, their education, their roommates, their love life—is to be present, guiding, and supportive, listening well and offering love, but not taking their problems on as your own.

One of my daughters will sometimes ask for a little advice and then do things her way, while the other asks for advice often. It was the day after the second anniversary of Richard's passing when Jazz learned she was pregnant. She was on birth control pills, so she was understandably astonished and upset.

I really couldn't believe it either, but as I held her while she cried and assured her that everything would be all right, I breathed very deeply. When she was calm, we sat down, woman-to-woman, and had a heart-to-heart talk. I told my daughter that this would be the greatest transition of her life, but I would be with her, backing her up, every step of the way. While she would be the mother, I would be there to support her 100 percent.

A few months back, I was speaking with a woman about her adult daughter, who was moving home at thirty-eight years of age. She told me that her daughter had struggled with drug and alcohol addiction, and was now in recovery. But this wasn't the first time her daughter had been in rehab, and the mother wasn't sure her daughter wouldn't relapse again. The woman looked at me and said, "This was supposed to be my time. I am supposed to be done with this phase of life. I finally just left my house for the first time in two months. I'm afraid of what might happen if I leave her for more than a night, but I can't babysit her for the rest of my life." I agreed: "No, you can't, and managing her life is not your job. She has to take responsibility for herself."

I've known parents of adult children who step in and pay off their kids' credit card bills, only to have them ring up the charges again. As moms, our instincts will always be to save our children. We can't help but want to isolate them from catastrophe. Just as we did when they were children, we can anticipate the consequences that come from their inexperience or their poor decisions. But the difference is, they aren't children any longer. It's more complicated now than just being their safe place to land. When our adult children have problems, we need to step back from a reactive emotional mindset and assess what actions may just be putting a Band-Aid on an issue that really instead should require them to make a major life adjustment. Sometimes growth only happens after there's been some pain. Sometimes, we need to show our love by what we *won't* do for our kids. It's how we help our children to make those final steps into full adulthood by owning their lives and choices, and developing resiliency in adverse circumstances.

While we don't want to abandon our adult kids when they are low, we have to come to a deep understanding within ourselves and separate their problems from our own. If we take their problems on, we are diluting their ability to grow into the adult person they are meant to be—someone who can live a full life and be fully responsible for their actions, outcomes, and dreams. Good things will happen for our children, and bad things will happen, too. This is the Life 101 curriculum for most people.

Your job as a mom is a lifetime one, but your role changes over time. As your kids grow up and turn eighteen, they will still need you, but not always in the same way they did when they were young. You are not the "mother duck" anymore, and they are certainly no longer ducklings. Allow them to fly on their own. Love, listen, support, and guide them when they ask, but stay detached from solving their issues and problems. Their problems belong to them. It's your time to step out, and it's their time to step up and become independent adults truly capable of living life on their own.

99

WHEN THINGS FALL APART

❀ This chapter could really be its own book. It is no small wonder that certain periods of our lives with children feel like especially difficult passages. These are times when we are going through transitions and changes ourselves, but simultaneously, so are our kids. It's no coincidence that the teenage years hit us like a ton of bricks. Our own lives are changing as radically as theirs. No wonder it's such a combustible time!

We look back at those first tender years when we had toddlers and we were building our lives and careers. It was an incredibly taxing time on us emotionally and physically, dealing with sleepless nights and long days at work, and caring at home for our small ones. But those years were also blessed by the joy and novelty of seeing this young life grow before our eyes. We were younger then, of course, and our energy—and rising prospects—was the fuel that somehow made the chaos and fatigue negotiable, and the small stuff of family legend later. When our kids began elementary school, our lives seemed to settle down into something that worked and ran smoothly. We established our routines; our children did their homework, did their scouts and sports, were excited about life and learning—and we were often left amazed that we'd created something from nothing but love.

Then, they enter puberty, and somehow we feel as though we've hit a wall. We are exhausted; we've lost confidence in ourselves, in our future, in our ability to mother with the wisdom and pleasure we once had. *What happened*, we ask ourselves. Nothing much—unless you notice that our own lives are convulsing, too. One might think that Nature is playing a terrible joke when we stop to realize that our kids' teenage years are taking place alongside the emergence of our own midlife issues that can exacerbate the stresses we feel with our children. Think about it: For many of us, we are for the first time confronting potentially serious health issues; we are dealing (some of us) with job loss or job change; our marriages may be falling apart as we've drifted away from our partner. We feel adrift and vaguely afraid that half of our lives are now behind us. While our kids are concerned about what college they will attend, we are worried about how we will pay for it. In other words, we are moving into a midlife crisis, just as our teens are moving into adolescence—which some would argue is, by definition, a crisis, too.

I've heard the story more than once about the mom who looks like she's Betty Crocker's granddaughter, but she's having an affair with the football coach of her son's team, and thinks she's in love. Truth is, she's in midlife crisis and she's as confused about her internal struggles and emotions as her son is about his changing body and hormones. We are questioning ourselves—our choices, and maybe everything we've ever held sacred—just at the time our teens are pushing the boundaries, developing into their own people with their own ideas. At a time when we thought we'd left behind the heavy, hands-on parenting our kids needed when they were younger, it appears they require more, not less, of our attention, and we're not prepared for it.

This is a time when our lives—ours and our kids'—are converging in new and ironic ways. We are each struggling with our identity, independent of one another, but we are a family—and what part of that is not connected? Our struggles may be more sophisticated than our children's, but often they aren't really that different from theirs—only the ante is. It's also ironic that at two of the busiest times of our lives—raising toddlers and teens—our careers often require the most from us, too. This is a time when we think our teens should be more independent than they are—but rebellion and testing you in every which way isn't the sort of helpful independence you had in mind. And so we labor to keep our eyes on the road and teach our kids to do the same thing. Unlike our children, who aren't supposed to have the answers but think they do, we are supposed to have all the answers, and yet we're fighting just to hold it all together.

It's helpful to anticipate that this period of change and disorder may be ahead, and to know that panic is not the answer. If it comes, you need to be alert to the turbulence around you, to wake up from your confusion and make sure that your priorities are straight, and not become blindsided by the backlash of midlife issues that can make you feel crazy.

You're not crazy—but you do need go inside to find the answers to your deeper questions. As you consider your life path, be certain that your family still needs you to stay present in theirs. There are time periods where we are birthing and rebirthing. There are times in our lives when we have to bear down just as we did when we pushed our babies out. When things fall apart, with good life practice and a broader focus, you can see that these periods will pass. And as you turn the corner as individuals, searching, you will come together again to cruise the horizon of better days ahead.

100

YOU JUST GOTTA ROLL

❀ Raising Jasmine and Kenna has been a great privilege. My children have called from me a deep purpose, and, in thousands of situations, have brought me into circumstances that have reflected who I really am in my inner core. They are my mirror, showing me all the good stuff, and, well, some of the stuff that's not so pretty, too.

As the heart of the home, we moms can heal the world with our love. Love creates its own ripple effect. It's truly astounding how powerful a mother's love can be, and what we can do with it. Most of us wouldn't see ourselves as prepared and able for such a big job, but we do it, day by day, and before we know it, the days take newborns from infancy into productive and happy adulthood. We give them life, and they change the world. It's pretty fantastic.

Now, looking back, I can clearly see the things I did right as a mom, and those things I wish I had done differently, too. I know there will come a day when I ask myself what they remember best about those years that flashed by like a meteor. Will they remember the times I lost my patience, or the times I found the right words and helped them through a difficult moment? Will they even remember what we gave them, or will they remember how we failed them? All I know is that I understand today that life is not a tidy box with a bow all tied up tightly and neatly, and that motherhood is certainly not that, either. But there is treasure in that box all the same: The treasure is all the small things that you did and overcame together, and these are the real gifts of life.

While I was writing this book, Jasmine learned she was pregnant. Not only that, an ultrasound indicated she was carrying twins! She was beyond devastated at the idea, because her goal is to finish school and pursue a career in nursing. Her son, Caden, is only twenty months old. While Jasmine sobbed, I had to laugh at the news and remind her that "Life just happens sometimes." Our best-laid plans are the ones that are made to be broken. Then, after she made the emotional and organizational adjustment to the idea of twins, Jazz was told that there had been a mistake. A new ultrasound revealed only one baby, a healthy boy. She is now elated, thinking that one infant baby and a two-year-old will be easy. (I will remember to remind her that she said this. Often.) It's all about perspective, isn't it?

Life surely is a roller coaster, and you can ride a roller coaster two ways. One is to let go and ride it in complete surrender, and the other is to brace yourself against the curves and try to stay in control. Life throws us some curveballs, especially with our kids. But the empowered mom knows when it's time to let go and just roll.

My measure of success as a mom is not keyed to anyone else's metric of how my kids have turned out. My measure of success is simply knowing I did the best I could, given any number of variables on any given day. To this day, I know I can't fix all of my kids' problems, and that we are all on a journey, living a process, holding hands together along the way.

As I roll into this next phase of life, I have room now to answer the question: What do I want to be when my kids grow up? As a single grandmother on the rising side of fifty, and with more room in my nest than I ever could have imagined, I still have the enthusiasm, vitality, and strength of a woman in her late thirties. I can rebirth into another life. I can reinvent the rest of my life with renewed passion, only this time my role as mother will not include that all-consuming responsibility. I will miss it, and I won't. I know I will experience all the joy, with far less burden. There's a time for everything—and it's more my time now.

Treasure the journey and the gifts of life and love—and no matter what, treasure and love all the children.

It's all unimaginably precious.

ACKNOWLEDGMENTS

First and foremost, I want to acknowledge my late husband, Richard Carlson, who made writing the Don't Sweat book series look so easy. Teaching happiness was his purpose, and writing about how to be happy, his passion. Many thanks and much love to him, always, for being my co-parent and partner for twenty-five years. I treasure an endless sea of memories I have with Richard that includes all the best stuff life has to offer in Love.

While it takes a village to raise a child, it seems the same can be said for me to finish this book! I would like to acknowledge an incredible team of supporters!

First, I'd like to thank my editors Leslie Wells and Susan Leon. A special thanks to my executive assistant, Lynden Tripp, who did a beautiful job as doula, supporting this project to its birth! Special thanks to my good friend and life/business coach, Steve Maraboli, who has helped me gather the reins of this great brand. My gratitude to Renny Madlena for his emotional support, and to Carole Foley-Stewart for sweating the small stuff for me, so I don't have to.

Deepest appreciation for the support from my friends who are expert "moms": Dana Dowell Windatt, TJ Nelson, Laura Hulburd, Simin Kaabi, Diana La Brecque, Nancy Katz, Melanie Desautels, Jane Carone, Lisa Marino, Kathy Fettke, Jeanine Stanley, Dana Hilmer, Mary Vesey, Alana Leigh, Maryanne Comaroto, and Judy Domenici.

A special thanks to my friends who are devoted to making this world a better place for all the children. Thanks to Rich Dutra and Yvonne St. John Dutra for your program, Challenge Day, and film documentary, *Teen Files*. And to Jennifer Seibel Newsom for bringing her amazing documentary *Miss Representation* to the public. These films hit chords of emotion in me that greatly impacted this book.

Thanks to my Femmamind group of wonderful women supporters: Queen of Self-Love and author, Christine Arylo; Wake-up Call Coach and author, Amy Ahlers; Relationship Astrologer extraordinaire and author, Carol Allen; and Spiritual Finance guru and author, Karen Russo.

All my love and appreciation to my daughters, Jasmine and Kenna, who have made it fun to be their mom, and so freely allow me to share our family experiences with the world!

RESOURCES

BOOKS

Catching Up or Leading the Way
Yong Zhao

Be the Hero You've Been Waiting For
Yvonne St. John Dutra and Rich Dutra St. John

Big Fat Lies
Amy Ahlers

Heart Broken Open
Kristine Carlson

Hindsight
Maryanne Comaroto

Odd Girl Out
Rachel Simmons

Raising Resilient Children
Robert Brooks, Ph.D.
Sam Goldstein, Ph.D.

Reality Bites Back
Jennifer Pozner

The Big Book of Parenting Solutions
Michele Borba, Ed.D.

The Good Life
Sherry Ackerman, Ph.D.

The Lolita Effect
Gigi Durham, Ph.D.

The Power of One
Life, the Truth, and Being Free
Steve Maraboli

The 7 Habits of Highly Effective Families
Stephen R. Covey

Women's Bodies, Women's Wisdom
Christiane Northrup, M.D.

Raising Mario Twice
Christine Sharmer

BOOKS BY RICHARD CARLSON, PH.D.

You Can Be Happy No Matter What
The Big Book of Small Stuff
Easier Than You Think
Shortcut Through Therapy
You Can Feel Good Again
Slowing Down to the Speed of Life

DOCUMENTARIES

Miss Representation
Jennifer Siebel Newsom
www.missrepresentation.org/home.html

Teen Files, Challenge Day
Yvonne St. John Dutra and Rich Dutra St. John
www.challengeday.org/videos.php

Race to Nowhere
Vicki Abeles
www.racetonowhere.com

ORGANIZATIONS AND WEBSITES

A Better Today, Inc.
Steve Maraboli
www.stevemaraboli.com

B Walker Ranch
A Working Ranch Day Program for Special Needs Adults
Jeanine Stanley
www.BWalkerRanch.org

Challenge Day
Yvonne St. John Dutra and Rich Dutra St. John
www.challengeday.org

Cultivating Radiance
Tamara Gerlach
tamaragerlach.com

Dare to Live You/Choosing Me before We
Christine Arylo
www.daretoliveyou.com

Emotional Freedom Technique/Tapping
Kate Winch
www.katewinch.com

It Gets Better Project
www.itgetsbetter.org

Joy of Mom
www.joyofmom.com

Sherry Ackerman, Ph.D.
www.sherryackerman.com

Take Back Family Time
Dana Hilmer
www.lifestylemom.com

The Money Keys
Karen Russo
www.themoneykeys.com/meetkarenrusso.html

Vedic Astrology
Carol Allen
www.carolallenastrology.com

Wake-Up Call Coaching/The Big Fat Lies Women Tell Themselves
Amy Ahlers
wakeupcallcoaching.com